Musicaliti Nursery: Run, Hop, Skip

FRANCES TURNBULL

Published by Musicaliti® Publishers
575 Tonge Moor Road, Bolton, BL2 3BN

Copyright © 2017 Musicaliti®
ISBN 978-1-907935-17-6

All rights reserved. No part of this publication may be reproduced, stored in a retrieval system, or transmitted by any means, mechanical, photocopying, recording or otherwise, without the prior permission of the copyright holder.

CONTENTS

	Introduction	v
	Curriculum Detail	vi
	What you will need	vii
	What it sounds like	viii
	Activity Planner	x
1	Swimming	13
2	Cycling	23
3	Running	33
4	Canoeing	43
5	Gymnastics	53
6	Tennis	63
7	Handouts	73
8	Musicaliti Characters	80
9	Make your own Rhythms	82

MUSICALITI NURSERY: RUN, HOP, SKIP
INTRODUCTION

SPACE is an acronym that we use to describe the elements in every Musicaliti® session.

Sing:
We sing before we play on the instruments, because:
Singing provides immediate feedback and shows understanding.

Play:
We play games and instruments every time, because:
Games are fun and easily hold attention because they depend on responding immediately!

Act:
We act out the story or characters, because:
Acting develops empathy and helps to develop subtle changes in dynamics like loud and quiet.

Create:
We create our own music, because:
Understanding and creating original music shows true musicality.

Explore:
We explore new ways to make sounds, because:
Improvisation is the ability to respond musically to a feeling or story.

SPACE statements are research-based reasons for the activities we do. Using the acronym SPACE, these areas highlight the essential areas of child development and provide an explanation of the benefits of the selected activities.

Social:
The welcoming greeting routine prepares children for a new activity as well as demonstrating a better way to start the day/session.

Physical:
Including whispering, speaking and singing allows children to experiment with communication.

Academic:
Developing sensitive listening helps children to respond better to instruction and detail.

Creative:
Teaching patterns develops children spatial planning and awareness.

Emotional:
Routine provides emotional security through knowing what to expect.

F S TURNBULL

Musicaliti® means learning for life

Musicaliti® is the complete creative curriculum for children from birth to 7.

Age	0-1 year	1-2 years	2-3 years	3-4 years	4-5 years	5-6 years	6-7 years
Awards	Red	Orange	Yellow	Green	Blue	Purple	Violet
Circle work	Sit and sway	Sit and tap knees	Hold hands and walk	Play circle games	Step forward and step back	Inner and outer circles	Dance with inner and outer circles
Line work	Roll over	Walk in pairs	Follow in a line	Follow in a spiral	Walk in line, create bridge	Walk in/out of spiral	Walk in line with partners
Completing the song	Show surprise	Continue song thru movement	Continue song vocally	Sing the last phrase	Sing the last 2 phrases	Sing the missing motif	Clap beat of missing motif
Listening work	Eyes follow movement	Eyes follow movement	Copy actions	Copy actions	Play partner games	Play partner games	Conduct songs in 2/4
Language work	Point at things	Point at body parts	Act song characters	Act song characters	Understand clever lyrics	Acting as different characters	Perform song in character
Instrument work	Shaking instruments	Tapping instruments	Drum and beater	Triangle and beater	Cymbal and beater	Glockenspiel (2 notes)	Ukulele (2 strings)
Pulse match	Clapping	Stamping	Flicking/ clicking	Hopping	Skipping	Patsching (knee tap)	Variety of methods
Rhythm match	Crotchet	Crotchet	Crotchet, quaver	Crotchet, quaver	Crotchet, quaver, dotted rhythm	Crotchet, quaver, dotted rhythm	Crotchet, quaver, dotted rhythm, minim
Interval match	Minor 3rd (A-F# or sol-mi)	Minor 3rd (A-F# or sol-mi)	Major 6th (B-D' or sol-la)	Perfect 5th (A-D' or sol-doh)	Major 3rd (F#-D or mi-doh)	Major 2nd (E-D or re-doh)	Octave (D"-D' or doh-doh')
Pitch match	Bouncing up (A) and down (F#)	Jumping up (A) and down (F#)	Clap (A) and hips (D)	Shoulders (B) to head (D')	Hips (F#) to toes (D)	Knees (E) to toes (D)	Overhead (D") to toes (D')
Singing	a'-a"	a'-a"	d'-b'	c'-c"	d'-d"	d'-d"	d'-d"
Songs in a year	3/5 songs	6/10 songs	11/20 songs	12/27 songs	16/35 songs	22/42 songs	28/50 songs
Weekly	10 min	10 min	15 min	20 min	30 min x 2	45 min	45 min

In every subject, we develop skills incrementally, from easy to complex. The same is true in music, so we use physical activity to introduce complex skills, from bouncing and rolling over, to walking and skipping, to writing music notation.

The Musicaliti® series provides activities to support the musical development of children from birth until they are physically strong and mentally experienced enough to hold and play musical instruments, in turn developing their other learning areas like maths and reading.

MUSICALITI NURSERY: RUN, HOP, SKIP

What you will need:

Weeks 1 and 2:
CD/iPod, scarves/ribbons, sticks, parachute, egg shakers, balls

Weeks 3 and 4:
CD/iPod, sandblocks, egg shakers, mixed instruments

Weeks 5 and 6:
CD/iPod, sticks, sandblocks, bells, triangles/cymbals, sticks, mixed instruments

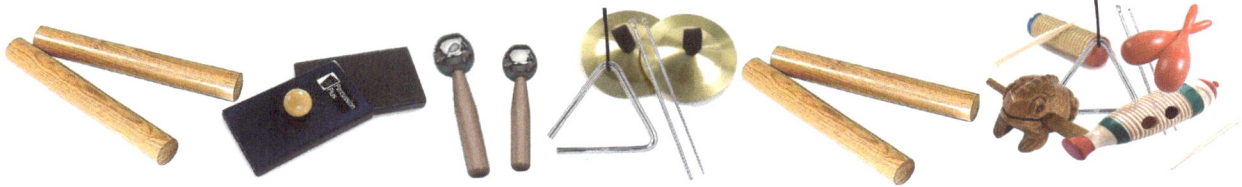

Weeks 7 and 8:
CD/iPod, triangles, drums, maracas, tambourine, parachute/blanket, mixed instruments

Weeks 9 and 10:
CD/iPod, hoops/boxes, pipes, scarves, bells

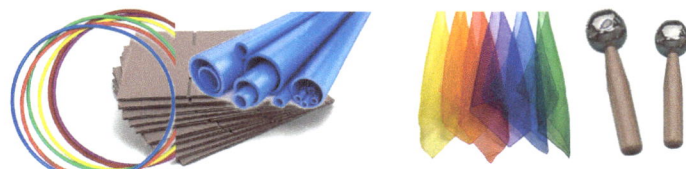

Weeks 11 and 12:
CD/iPod, balls, ukulele, boxes, glockenspiel, mixed instruments

What it sounds like:

What is a beat (or pulse)?
In music, a beat is the ongoing tap or clap in a song. It can be thought of as the 'heartbeat' of the song because this is what keeps the song going, usually by the low instruments. You can hear the beat of any song by walking to it. It is even-paced, usually taking the same length of time as the next tap or clap, and does not usually match the words or tune of the song. It can even sound a little boring, e.g. 'twinkle, twinkle, little star' or 'bee-bee-bee-bee'.

What is a rhythm?
In music, a rhythm is a group of notes together. Sometimes it is repeated by percussion instruments (shaking/tapping/scraping), so that all through the song, you hear 'cup of tea - cup of tea -', or like the insect notes below, 'spider-bee, spider-bee'. It is also the tune or words/lyrics of the song, e.g. 'twinkle, twinkle, little star' or 'spider-spider-spider-bee'.

NOTE/RHYTHM (basic)	MOVEMENT	WORD SOUND	INSECT PICTURE
semibreve / whole note	ve-ry slow walk 1 - - - *long*	4 counts snai-ai-ai-il	
minim / half note	slow walk 1 - *long*	2 counts wo-rm	
crotchet / quarter note	walk 1 *step*	1 count bee	
quaver / eighth note	jog-ging 1-2 *step-step*	1 count spi-der	
semiquaver / sixteenth note	jog-ging quick-ly 1 - 2 - 3 - 4 *short-short-short-short*	1 count ca-ter-pil-lar	

MUSICALITI NURSERY: RUN, HOP, SKIP

What it sounds like:

Why move to music?
In many cultures, the word music means 'dance and sound', because in all cultures, music composers are inspired by movement. When we can experience a rhythm or a beat, we learn it inside-out, and are able to repeat it over again without needing to think about it. Moving to music is also the most effective behaviour control, demanding the attention of all faculties, as well as giving the teacher immediate feedback on individual student understanding.

Why use pictures and words?
Using pictures, words or even rhythm sounds (ta, ti-ti etc) are bridges to understanding notation, and just as we all have different learning styles, these are yet another form of bridge. You may find children that prefer to use notation straight away, or prefer alternative bridges that don't hold specific meaning - the only time it is wrong is if it leads to incorrect or inaccurate understanding, which is seen instantly in the singing, playing or performance of the song.

NOTE/RHYTHM (basic)	MOVEMENT	WORD SOUND	INSECT PICTURE
dotted quaver semiquaver (dotted eighth note sixteenth note)	skip-ty 1 - 2 *long-short*	1 count bee-tle	beetle
semiquaver dotted quaver (sixteenth note dotted eighth note)	gal-lop 1 - 2 *short-long*	1 count the-ant	ant
triplet	tri-ple run 1 - 2 - 3 *jog-jog-jog*	1 count but-ter-fly	butterfly
quaver-semiquaver-semiquaver (eighth note sixteenth notes)	jog quick-ly 1 - 2 - 3 *long-short-short*	1 count ham - bur-ger	hamburger
semiquaver-semiquaver-quaver (sixteenth notes eighth note)	quick-ly jog 1 - 2 3 *short-short-long*	1 count sau-sa-ges	sausages

F S TURNBULL

Run Hop Skip Activity Planner

Nursery

Activity	Week 1:	Week 2:	Week 3:	Week 4:	Week 5:	Week 6:
Hello Song	Whispering Voice	Whispering Voice	Whispering Voice	Whispering Voice	Whispering Voice	Whispering Voice
Physical Warm Up	Round the garden	Round the garden	Pop goes the weasel	Pop goes the weasel	Wee Willie Winkie	Wee Willie Winkie
Vocal Warm Up	Round and round	Round and round	Circle right	Circle right	Here we come	Here we come
Pattern Dance	Old Brass Wagon	Old Brass Wagon	Snail snail	Snail snail	Down came my friend	Down came my friend
Instrument Play	Bounce High	Bounce High	Babylon	Babylon	Jolly Miller	Jolly Miller
Story	History of swimming	History of swimming	History of cycling	History of cycling	History of athletics	History of athletics
Body Percussion	The Rule	*	*	*	*	*
Rhythm	*	Also Sprach Zarathustra	*	*	*	*
Tempo	*	*	Lift Motif	*	*	*
Dynamics	*	*	*	Danse Macabre - I	*	*
Free Dance	*	*	*	*	Ecossaise in E-flat	*
Instrument Pass	*	*	*	*	*	Hustle
Craft ideas	Balloon swimmer	Paper plate pool	Pipecleaner cyclist	Paper plate bicycle	Pipecleaner athlete	Painted footprints
Goodbye Song	Goodbye my friends	Goodbye my friends	Goodbye my friends	Goodbye my friends	Goodbye my friends	Goodbye my friends

* The **separate** teaching CD matches the lesson plan printed above, however this may not be suitable for every group. The instrumental recording, i.e. 'The Rule', can be used for the activity suggested (i.e. 'body percussion') or for any other aspect of musical development (i.e. rhythm, tempo, dynamics, free dance, instrument pass) at the teacher's discretion.

MUSICALITI NURSERY: RUN, HOP, SKIP

Run Hop Skip Activity Planner

Activity	Week 7:	Week 8:	Week 9:	Week 10:	Week 11:	Week 12:
Hello Song	Whispering Voice	Whispering Voice	Whispering Voice	Whispering Voice	Whispering Voice	Whispering Voice
Physical Warm Up	Row your boat	Row your boat	Ring a Rosies	Ring a Rosies	Old brass wagon	Old brass wagon
Vocal Warm Up	Rock a bye baby	Rock a bye baby	What shall we do?	What shall we do?	Bounce high	Bounce high
Pattern Dance	See Saw	See Saw	All around the buttercup	All around the buttercup	Riding in a buggy	Riding in a buggy
Instrument Play	This way Valerie	This way Valerie	Skip to my Lou	Skip to my Lou	Rover red Rover	Rover red Rover
Story	History of canoeing	History of canoeing	History of gymnastics	History of gymnastics	History of tennis	History of tennis
Body Percussion	Dance of sugar plum	*	*	*	*	*
Rhythm	*	Digya	*	*	*	*
Tempo	*	*	Egmont Overture F	*	*	*
Dynamics	*	*	*	Thaxted	*	*
Free Dance	*	*	*	*	Also Sprach Zarathustra	*
Instrument Pass	*	*	*	*	*	The rule
Craft ideas	Butter dish canoe	Pipecleaner paddle	Pipecleaner gymnast	Dancing ribbons	Paper plate tennis raquet	Balloon tennis
Goodbye Song	Goodbye my friends	Goodbye my friends	Goodbye my friends	Goodbye my friends	Goodbye my friends	Goodbye my friends

* The **separate** teaching CD matches the lesson plan printed above, however this may not be suitable for every group. The instrumental recording, i.e. 'Dance of Sugar Plum', can be used for the activity suggested (i.e. 'body percussion') or for any other aspect of musical development (i.e. rhythm, tempo, dynamics, free dance, instrument pass) at the teacher's

1 Swimming

Olympics

The Olympics are held every 4 years in different countries. This syllabus invites adults to look at the last Olympic results of their own country or countries represented by their children, and recognise the highest achieving individuals. Children may find the winners stories interesting, particularly finding out more about their childhood start in the sport, their family circumstances growing up, and outside jobs or interests.

Swimming

Swimming has been an Olympic sport since 1896. Competitions used to be held in rivers, lakes and even in the icy Mediterranean, where swimmers were sailed out by boat and had to swim back to the shore.

Swimming pools have changed a lot and are now temperature-controlled. Some are even designed to reduce waves.

Although swimming has been included for a long time, women have only been allowed to compete since 1912, and both men and women can now take part in 16 events using 4 different strokes. Swimmers can use freestyle for distances ranging from 50 to 1500 metres. Backstroke, butterfly and breakstroke can only be used for 100m and 200m. Each race has a maximum of 8 swimmers.

Circles

Songs included in this chapter involve giving the children the experience of walking in a circle. With different variations of circular dances, having children stand in a circle allows them to experience their own personal space. Getting used to walking and stopping, performing actions and then joining up together to continue walking again develops the concept of sequencing and co-operative teamwork.

F S TURNBULL

Whispering Voice

Hello Song

What you will need:

Masking tape music spots for sitting places.
Instruments and equipment out of reach.
Cover distractions with fabric.

Welcome children to Musicaliti!
Shall we practice our whispering voices:
(whisper) Do you have your whispering voice?
Let's practice our speaking voices:
(speak aloud) Do you have your speaking voice?
What about your singing voice:
(sing) Do you have your singing voice?
I think we're ready to begin!

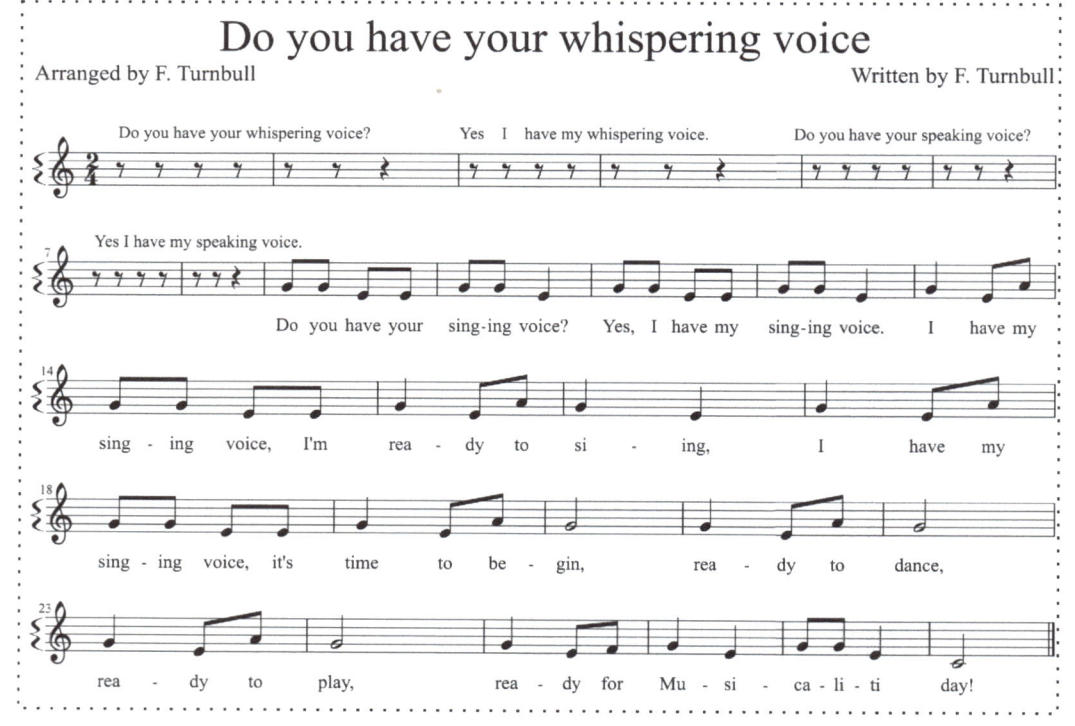

Nursery Week 1&2

SPACE Statement

Social: Socially we stand and talk to friends in a circle, allowing us to interact with everyone equally - sitting in a circle does the same.

Physical: Modelling actions or tapping a beat enhances learning by using more senses.

Academic: Introducing new words develops vocabulary as well as other subjects like geography, history and science.

Creative: Exploring instruments and finding different ways to play them develops problem solving ideas.

Emotional: Singing together calms people by regulating the heartbeat.

MUSICALITI NURSERY: RUN, HOP, SKIP

Nursery Week 1 & 2

Round the garden
Physical Warm Up

What you will need:

Week 1 & 2:   Scarves/ribbons

Focus: Creating circular movements

Developing fine motor co-ordination using gross motor movements, our focus is creating circular movements to the rhythm of the song.

> We're singing about swimming today!
> When we swim, our arms go around.
> Let's make our arms go around:
> round, round, round, round
> Let's draw a circle on our hand with our finger:
> round and round and round and round
> Now let's swap hands:
> round and round and round and round
>
> Can your fingers go for a walk?
> Let's walk from your hand up your arm:
> walk, walk, walk, walk, walk, walk, walk, walk
> Let's walk from your knee down your leg:
> walk, walk, walk, walk, walk, walk, walk, walk
> Now let's sing, drawing our circle with scarves/ribbons!

SPACE Statement

Social: Socially we stand and talk to friends in a circle, allowing us to interact with everyone equally - sitting in a circle does the same.

Physical: Modelling actions or tapping a beat enhances learning by using more senses.

Academic: Introducing new words develops vocabulary as well as other subjects like geography, history and science.

Creative: Exploring instruments and finding different ways to play them develops problem solving ideas.

Emotional: Singing together calms people by regulating the heartbeat.

Round and round the garden — Musolympics
Arranged by F. Turnbull — Traditional

Round and round the gar-den like a ted-dy bear, one step, two steps, ti-ckle you un-der there!

Nursery Week 1&2

Round and round
Vocal Warm Up

What you will need:

Week 1:   Walking in a circle
Week 2:   Tap sticks together

Focus: Walking sideways to the crotchet beat.

Taking a step for every beat reinforces both the length of the crotchet as well as the continuous beat of music. Rolling or walking sideways adds a new dimension to children's movement signature, giving them more ideas on how to move confidently and creatively.

Lots of things go round, like arms in swimming.

Let's stand up in a circle. Are you holding hands?

Let's walk around:
round, round, round, round, round and stop
Let's go the other way:
round, round, round, round, round and stop
This is how wheels and grinders go around
to make flour for bread.
Let's walk around as we sing!

SPACE Statement

Social:
Socially we stand and talk to friends in a circle, allowing us to interact with everyone equally - sitting in a circle does the same.

Physical:
Modelling actions or tapping a beat enhances learning by using more senses.

Academic:
Introducing new words develops vocabulary as well as other subjects like geography, history and science.

Creative:
Exploring instruments and finding different ways to play them develops problem solving ideas.

Emotional:
Singing together calms people by regulating the heartbeat.

Round and Round
Traditional — Musical Munchies — Arranged by F. Turnbull

Round and round the wheel goes round, as it goes the corn is ground.

MUSICALITI NURSERY: RUN, HOP, SKIP

Nursery Week 1&2

Old Brass Wagon
Pattern Dance

What you will need:

Week 1 and 2:   Movement and parachute

Focus: Maintaining the pulse

We've been playing circle games, so let's play another!

Standing up together in a circle, let's walk to the left:
walk, walk, walk, walk, walk, walk, walk and stop
Now let's walk to the right:
walk, walk, walk, walk, walk, walk, walk and stop
Can you crouch down? Now stand up!
And crouch down! And stand up!
Now let's all walk in towards the middle.
And out. And in. And back out!

SPACE Statement

Social: Socially we stand and talk to friends in a circle, allowing us to interact with everyone equally - sitting in a circle does the same.

Physical: Modelling actions or tapping a beat enhances learning by using more senses.

Academic: Introducing new words develops vocabulary as well as other subjects like geography, history and science.

Creative: Exploring instruments and finding different ways to play them develops problem solving ideas.

Emotional: Singing together calms people by regulating the heartbeat.

Nursery Week 1&2

SPACE Statement

Social: Socially we stand and talk to friends in a circle, allowing us to interact with everyone equally - sitting in a circle does the same.

Physical: Modelling actions or tapping a beat enhances learning by using more senses.

Academic: Introducing new words develops vocabulary as well as other subjects like geography, history and science.

Creative: Exploring instruments and finding different ways to play them develops problem solving ideas.

Emotional: Singing together calms people by regulating the heartbeat.

Bounce High
Instrumental Play

What you will need:

Week 1:   Egg shakers

Week 2:   Soft balls

Focus: Shaking the pulse

In the first week the children shake the eggs to the pulse: **1-2-3-4, 1-2-3-4**. In the second week, they roll the balls to each other, aiming at rolling for the length of the line.

When we move our hand in water,
it feels like it stops us moving too quickly.
Let's use these egg shakers,
to keep the beat of this next song,
but without shaking them too quickly!
Next time we may use a ball
to roll to each other,
but not too quickly!
Today, let's shake the eggs to the beat!

Roll here

Traditional

Roll here, roll there, roll the ball to Leices-ter Square, Roll here, roll there, roll the ball to Leices-ter Square

Bounce high, bounce low, bounce the ball to Shi-loh, bounce high, bounce low, bounce the ball to Shi-loh!

MUSICALITI NURSERY: RUN, HOP, SKIP

Nursery Week 1&2

Swimming
Story/Investigation

SPACE Statement

What you will need:

Week 1 and 2:   Pictures and characters

* Reading each line slowly, encourage children to share their ideas.

Are you ready to listen?
Each week learn about an olympic sport.
Have you been swimming?
Let's rub our ears and get them ready to listen.

> Swimming has been an Olympic sport since 1896.
> Competitions used to be held in rivers, lakes
> and even in the icy Mediterranean,
> where swimmers were sailed out by boat
> and had to swim back to the shore.
> Swimming pools have changed a lot and are now
> temperature-controlled,
> Some are even designed to reduce waves.
> Although swimming has been included for a long time,
> women have only been allowed to compete since 1912,
> and both men and women can now take part
> in 16 events using 4 different strokes.
> Swimmers can use freestyle for
> distances ranging from 50 to 1500 metres.
> Backstroke, butterfly and breakstroke
> can only be used for 100m and 200m.
> Each race has a maximum of 8 swimmers.

Social: Socially we stand and talk to friends in a circle, allowing us to interact with everyone equally - sitting in a circle does the same.

Physical: Modelling actions or tapping a beat enhances learning by using more senses.

Academic: Introducing new words develops vocabulary as well as other subjects like geography, history and science.

Creative: Exploring instruments and finding different ways to play them develops problem solving ideas.

Emotional: Singing together calms people by regulating the heartbeat.

F S TURNBULL

Nursery Week 1&2

SPACE Statement

Social: Socially we stand and talk to friends in a circle, allowing us to interact with everyone equally - sitting in a circle does the same.

Physical: Modelling actions or tapping a beat enhances learning by using more senses.

Academic: Introducing new words develops vocabulary as well as other subjects like geography, history and science.

Creative: Exploring instruments and finding different ways to play them develops problem solving ideas.

Emotional: Singing together calms people by regulating the heartbeat.

Swimming
Instrumental

What you will need:

Week 1: No equipment required
Track length: 0.57 (The Rule, K.MacCleod)

This time is for creative expression without talking. Using body percussion, explore tapping the body (head, ears, shoulders, tummy, toes), claps and patches (knee taps), steps and stomps. Starting from head to toe helps in preventing repetition. The music is in 4/4 time, so tap in time to the music and only change to a new movement after a count of 4. Read the Swimming paragraph for movement inspiration.

Focus on contrasts like loud/quiet, high/low, fast/slow.

Week 2: No equipment required
Track length: 1.26 (Also Sprach Zarathustra, K. MacCleod)

This time is for creative expression without talking. Move in time or play instruments to the tune that you hear. Beat is the regular timing of the song, while rhythm follows the song words or tune, so choose whether to play to the beat or the rhythm of the song. Look at pictures about Swimming for movement inspiration.

It's time to listen to music
and find a creative way to respond.
Be sure to listen to how the music sounds,
whether it is high or low, quick or slow,
and try to copy it.
Let's find lots of different ways
to respond to the music.

Nursery Week 1 & 2

Goodbye

Goodbye Song

What you will need:

Week 1 and 2:   Sit in circle to sing goodbye.

The recording can be used when singing to younger children who won't sing back yet. Stop after "but now it's time to say" so that you can sing to each child, and wait for them to sing back their response. This is a perfect opportunity to determine whether children are singing in tune on their own.

If stickers have been used as rewards for behaviour during the session, this is also the time to ensure that each child receives a sticker, showing each child that you value them equally.

> What an exciting day we've had,
> playing games about swimming!
> It's time to go, so let's get our
> waving hands ready
> as we get ready to sing goodbye.

SPACE Statement

Social: Socially we stand and talk to friends in a circle, allowing us to interact with everyone equally - sitting in a circle does the same.

Physical: Modelling actions or tapping a beat enhances learning by using more senses.

Academic: Introducing new words develops vocabulary as well as other subjects like geography, history and science.

Creative: Exploring instruments and finding different ways to play them develops problem solving ideas.

Emotional: Singing together calms people by regulating the heartbeat.

2 Cycling

Olympics

The Olympics are held every 4 years in different countries. This syllabus invites adults to look at the last Olympic results of their own country or countries represented by their children, and recognise the highest achieving individuals. Children may find the winners stories interesting, particularly finding out more about their childhood start in the sport, their family circumstances growing up, and outside jobs or interests.

Cycling

Cycling has been an Olympic sport since 1896. Bicycles were invented in 1871 and they were called Penny Farthings because the front wheel was much larger than the back one - this actually made them quite dangerous. There are now four types of cycling competitions: road, track, mountain biking and BMX.

Track cyclists ride around a track shaped like a funnel at 42 degrees, called a velodrome, which makes the bikes go faster.

Some competitions involve a team of two, where they take turns to race, called a Madison. In the Kierin, a motor bike leads the riders until the last 600m. The Olympic sprint is where teams have to catch up to each other.

Circle dances

Circle dances have been around for centuries, so introducing them in the early years helps to share the history of society. Circle dances are great teaching tools, as they rely on informal learning techniques in a non-confrontational environment, teaching children about rules and timing in order to play successfully. Circle dances help children to develop spatial awareness through proprioception, making them less likely to be clumsy, so move more accurately without tripping, dropping or spilling. Finally, the introduction to shapes through gross motor movement makes fine motor co-ordination more likely to be successful. By physically experiencing a circle, children are more likely to recognise and ultimately draw a circle.

Nursery Week 3&4

Whispering Voice

Hello Song

What you will need:

Masking tape music spots for sitting places.
Instruments and equipment out of reach.
Cover distractions with fabric.

Welcome children to Musicaliti!
Shall we practise our whispering voices:
(whisper) Do you have your whispering voice?
Let's practise our speaking voices:
(speak aloud) Do you have your speaking voice?
What about your singing voice:
(sing) Do you have your singing voice?
I think we're ready to begin!

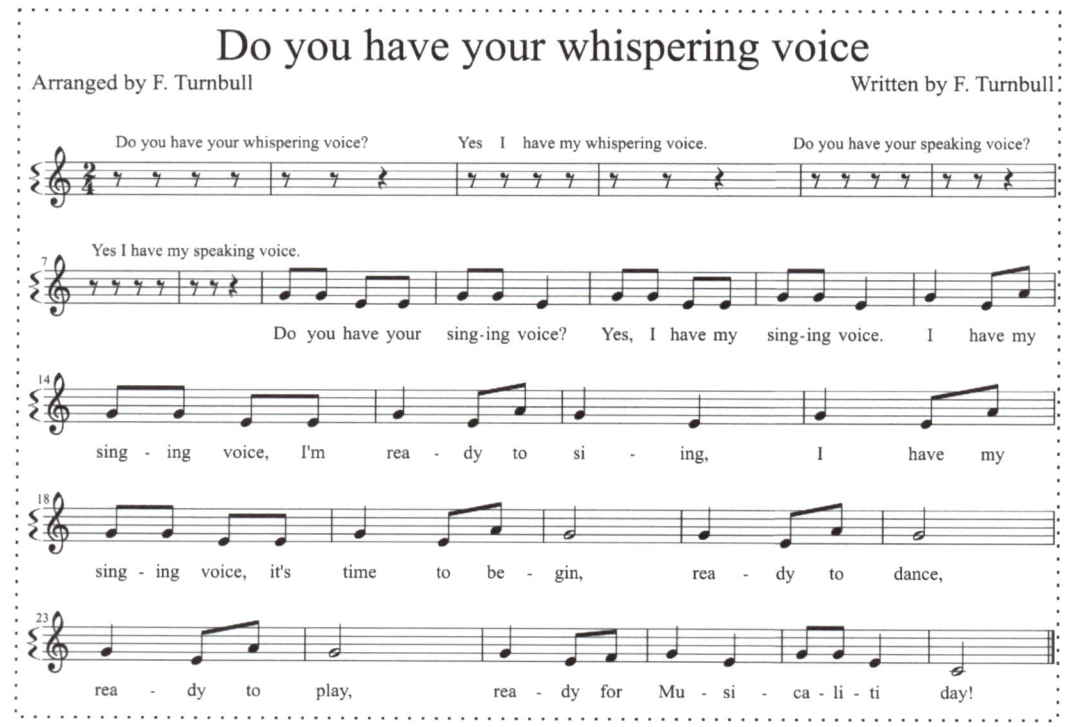

SPACE Statement

Social: Socially we stand and talk to friends in a circle, allowing us to interact with everyone equally - sitting in a circle does the same.

Physical: Modelling actions or tapping a beat enhances learning by using more senses.

Academic: Introducing new words develops vocabulary as well as other subjects like geography, history and science.

Creative: Exploring instruments and finding different ways to play them develops problem solving ideas.

Emotional: Singing together calms people by regulating the heartbeat.

MUSICALITI NURSERY: RUN, HOP, SKIP

Nursery Week 3&4

Pop goes the weasel

Physical Warm Up

What you will need:

Week 3: Sandblocks
Week 4: Changing direction in a circle

Focus: Last line

This week we emphasise the last phrase in the music. As the line begins with "Pop!", we simply choose a different way to play as we sing the last line. In the 4th week, walking in a circle, we change direction at "Pop!"

When we ride a bicycle, our feet go round and round,
like we're walking: pedal, pedal, pedal, pedal.
These instruments are called sandblocks,
because they have a rough, sandy bottom.
We can tap them together like this: tap, tap, tap, tap
We can also rub them together: rub, rub, rub, rub
We could tap the handles: tap, tap, tap, tap
We could rub the floor: rub, rub, rub, rub
We could even tap them against our friends' blocks!
Let's find a way to play them, and then change
to something else when we sing
"Pop! Goes the weasel!"

SPACE Statement

Social: Socially we stand and talk to friends in a circle, allowing us to interact with everyone equally - sitting in a circle does the same.

Physical: Modelling actions or tapping a beat enhances learning by using more senses.

Academic: Introducing new words develops vocabulary as well as other subjects like geography, history and science.

Creative: Exploring instruments and finding different ways to play them develops problem solving ideas.

Emotional: Singing together calms people by regulating the heartbeat.

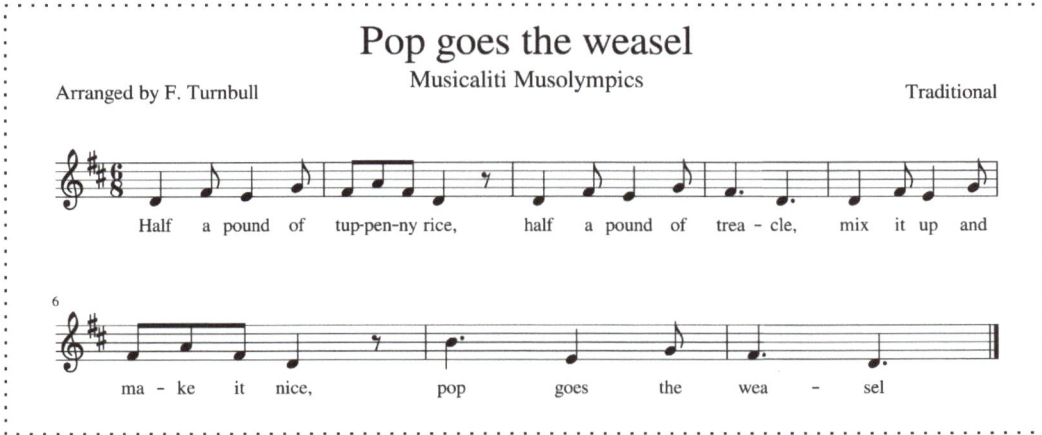

Nursery Week 3&4

Circle right
Vocal Warm Up

What you will need:

Week 3 and 4: Circle dance

Focus: Spatial awareness, last line

This song develops co-ordination, as children develop their ability to keep their distance whilst walking in a circle and singing – changing actions in the last line.

What shape are bicycle wheels?
That's right, they are round circles!
Let's stand up in a circle and go around as we sing our song.
We'll have to listen well, as we're going to shake our hands on the last line when we sing, "shake them 'simmons down!"
Shall we practise that?
"Shake them 'simmons down!"
A bit later, all the boys have to go
the middle of the circle and then back.
Then it's the girls turn to go the middle and back.
And then we, "shake them 'simmons down!"

SPACE Statement

Social: Socially we stand and talk to friends in a circle, allowing us to interact with everyone equally – sitting in a circle does the same.

Physical: Modelling actions or tapping a beat enhances learning by using more senses.

Academic: Introducing new words develops vocabulary as well as other subjects like geography, history and science.

Creative: Exploring instruments and finding different ways to play them develops problem solving ideas.

Emotional: Singing together calms people by regulating the heartbeat.

MUSICALITI NURSERY: RUN, HOP, SKIP

Nursery Week 3&4

Snail snail

Pattern Dance

What you will need:

Week 3:   Egg shakers

Week 4:   None

Focus: Rhythm, spiral shape

In the 3rd week, we focus on shaking the egg shakers to the beat of the words, slow-slow-slow-slow, quicker-quicker-quicker-quick. In the 4th week, hold hands in a long line and lead the children into a tight spiral, perhaps with an extension into maths shapes and relationships.

When we first start riding bicycles or tricycles,
we go quite slowly.
Suddenly, as we get better at riding,
we go quicker and quicker!
Let's shake our eggs like we've just started learning to ride:
slow-slow-slow-slow
And now, we're really good at riding our bikes:
quicker-quicker-quicker-quick!
Next week, we'll turn ourselves into a snail shell,
holding hands in a long, long line.

SPACE Statement

Social: Socially we stand and talk to friends in a circle, allowing us to interact with everyone equally - sitting in a circle does the same.

Physical: Modelling actions or tapping a beat enhances learning by using more senses.

Academic: Introducing new words develops vocabulary as well as other subjects like geography, history and science.

Creative: Exploring instruments and finding different ways to play them develops problem solving ideas.

Emotional: Singing together calms people by regulating the heartbeat.

Snail, snail
Musicaliti Musolympics
Arranged by F. Turnbull   Traditional

Snail, snail, snail, snail, creep a-round and round and round.

Nursery Week 3&4

Babylon
Instrument Play

What you will need:

Week 3 and 4:   Mixed instruments

Focus: Turn-taking, listening

In orchestras, in conversations, in life, we need to take turns and listen before we reply. This game develops listening skills as children sing and play, and wait for the other group before they can respond.

Let's sit in two lines opposite each other.
One side can use metal instruments, the other side, woods.
Let's hear the metals tap eight times:
tap, tap, tap, tap, tap, tap, tap, tap
Let's hear the woods tap eight times:
tap, tap, tap, tap, tap, tap, tap tap
That was great! Now let's swap over,
and get ready to sing our song.

SPACE Statement

Social: Socially we stand and talk to friends in a circle, allowing us to interact with everyone equally - sitting in a circle does the same.

Physical: Modelling actions or tapping a beat enhances learning by using more senses.

Academic: Introducing new words develops vocabulary as well as other subjects like geography, history and science.

Creative: Exploring instruments and finding different ways to play them develops problem solving ideas.

Emotional: Singing together calms people by regulating the heartbeat.

MUSICALITI NURSERY: RUN, HOP, SKIP

Cycling
Story/investigation

Nursery Week 3&4

SPACE Statement

What you will need:

Week 3 and 4: Pictures and characters

* Reading each line slowly, encourage children to act out the story.

Are you ready to listen?
Each week learn about an olympic sport.
Have you been cycling?
Let's rub our ears and get them ready to listen.

Cycling has been an Olympic sport since 1896.
Bicycles were invented in 1871
and they were called Penny Farthings
because the front wheel was much larger than the back one -
this actually made them quite dangerous.

There are now four types of cycling competitions:
road, track, mountain biking and BMX.

Track cyclists ride around a track shaped like a funnel at 42 degrees,
called a velodrome, which makes the bikes go faster.
Some competitions involve a team of two,
where they take turns to race, called a Madison.
In the Kierin, a motor bike leads the riders until the last 600m.
The Olympic sprint is where teams have to
catch up to each other.

Social: Socially we stand and talk to friends in a circle, allowing us to interact with everyone equally - sitting in a circle does the same.

Physical: Modelling actions or tapping a beat enhances learning by using more senses.

Academic: Introducing new words develops vocabulary as well as other subjects like geography, history and science.

Creative: Exploring instruments and finding different ways to play them develops problem solving ideas.

Emotional: Singing together calms people by regulating the heartbeat.

Nursery Week 3&4

SPACE Statement

Cycling
Instrumental

What you will need:

Week 3: No equipment required
Track length: 0.44 (Lift Motif, K.MaccCleod)

This time is for creative expression without talking. Walk when the music starts slowly and clap as music gets quicker. Go back to walking as the music slows down. We are showing that the change in tempo (speed) changes the mood of the music: slow music is calm, fast music is intense. Read the Cycling paragraph for movement inspiration.

Contrasting feet with hands is easier than fast/slow walking or clapping.

Week 4: No equipment required
Track length: 0.33 (Danse Macabre-Isolated, K. MacCleod)

This time is for creative expression without talking. Demonstrate long steps, quick jogging, walking and stopping. Emphasise the different lengths of notation. Look at pictures about Cycling for movement inspiration.

Focus on high/low contrasts by reaching up or down as appropriate.

It's time to listen to music
and find a creative way to respond.
Be sure to listen to how the music sounds,
whether it is high or low, quick or slow,
and try to copy it.
Let's find lots of different ways
to respond to the music.

Social: Socially we stand and talk to friends in a circle, allowing us to interact with everyone equally - sitting in a circle does the same.

Physical: Modelling actions or tapping a beat enhances learning by using more senses.

Academic: Introducing new words develops vocabulary as well as other subjects like geography, history and science.

Creative: Exploring instruments and finding different ways to play them develops problem solving ideas.

Emotional: Singing together calms people by regulating the heartbeat.

MUSICALITI NURSERY: RUN, HOP, SKIP

Nursery Week 3&4

Goodbye

Goodbye Song

What you will need:

Week 1 and 2:   Sit in circle to sing goodbye.

The recording can be used when singing to younger children who won't sing back yet. Stop after "but now it's time to say" so that you can sing to each child, and wait for them to sing back their response. This is a perfect opportunity to determine whether children are singing in tune on their own.

If stickers have been used as rewards for behaviour during the session, this is also the time to ensure that each child receives a sticker, showing each child that you value them equally.

What an exciting day we've had,
pretending to cycle!
It's time to go, so let's get our
waving hands ready
as we get ready to sing goodbye.

SPACE Statement

Social: Socially we stand and talk to friends in a circle, allowing us to interact with everyone equally - sitting in a circle does the same.

Physical: Modelling actions or tapping a beat enhances learning by using more senses.

Academic: Introducing new words develops vocabulary as well as other subjects like geography, history and science.

Creative: Exploring instruments and finding different ways to play them develops problem solving ideas.

Emotional: Singing together calms people by regulating the heartbeat.

3 Running

Olympics

The Olympics are held every 4 years in different countries. This syllabus invites adults to look at the last Olympic results of their own country or countries represented by their children, and recognise the highest achieving individuals. Children may find the winners stories interesting, particularly finding out more about their childhood start in the sport, their family circumstances growing up, and outside jobs or interests.

Athletics

Athletics was the first sport to be held at the Olympics. Since 776BC, running has been a large part of European fairs. Other examples of athletics can be found in the Irish Tailteann and Scotlands' Highland Games.

Women were first included in the sport in 1928. Now they compete in almost as many programmes as men.

Historically, American men have been the top champions, challenged only by the USSR and East Germany. Now many Caribbean countries are challenging them, while Olympians from African states dominate the distance events.

Passing the Baton

As a music session, this type of game helps children to see how a piece of music is arranged and performed. Usually starting with one or a few instruments, a music piece is built up traditionally perhaps with strings, then woodwind, percussion and brass. In popular music, this may be percussion (drums), strings (including piano, guitar), and woodwind. At different times, one or more instrument group may not be included, creating different moods towards the message of the song. Simplifying this, we can use different instruments groups to represent different song elements, and by taking turns, we can feel the mood that is created, and the easiest descriptors are "happy" or "sad".

Nursery Week 5 & 6

Whispering Voice

Hello Song

What you will need:

Masking tape music spots for sitting places.
Instruments and equipment out of reach.
Cover distractions with fabric.

Welcome children to Musicaliti!
Shall we practise our whispering voices:
(whisper) Do you have your whispering voice?
Let's practise our speaking voices:
(speak aloud) Do you have your speaking voice?
What about your singing voice:
(sing) Do you have your singing voice?
I think we're ready to begin!

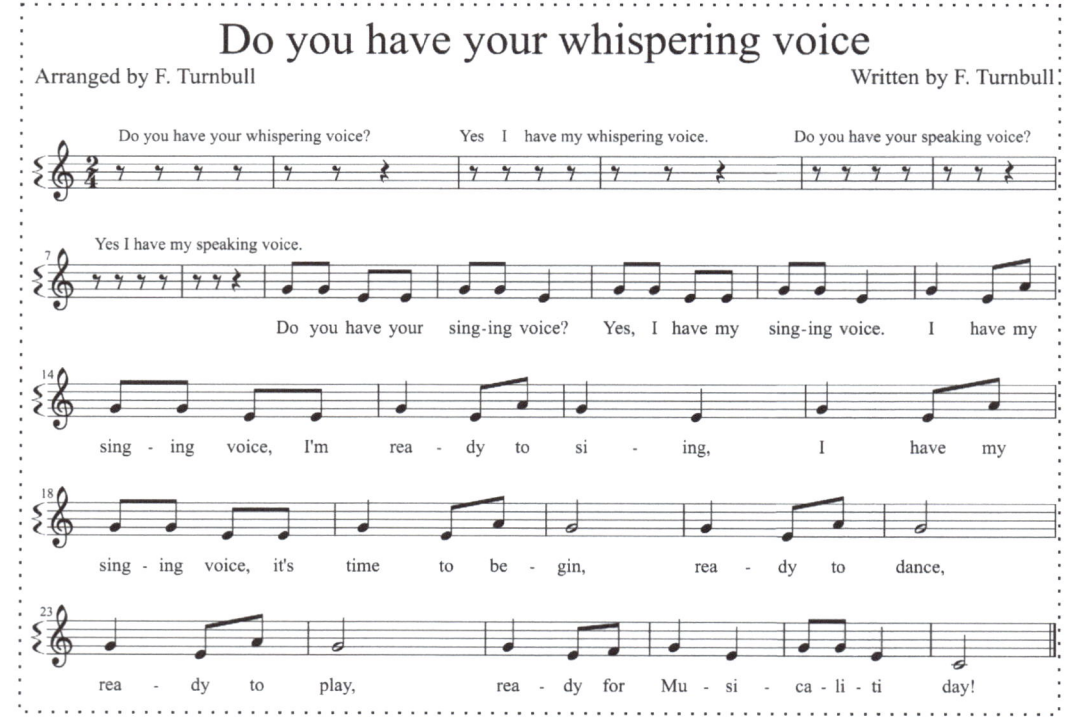

SPACE Statement

Social: Socially we stand and talk to friends in a circle, allowing us to interact with everyone equally - sitting in a circle does the same.

Physical: Modelling actions or tapping a beat enhances learning by using more senses.

Academic: Introducing new words develops vocabulary as well as other subjects like geography, history and science.

Creative: Exploring instruments and finding different ways to play them develops problem solving ideas.

Emotional: Singing together calms people by regulating the heartbeat.

MUSICALITI NURSERY: RUN, HOP, SKIP

Nursery Week 5&6

Wee Willie Winkie

Physical Warm Up

What you will need:

Week 5 & 6 :   4 different types of instruments

Focus: Phrasing

Just as language has phrasing broken up by punctuation, music has sound broken up by silence. Often in songs, these breaks occur at the end of a line. In this song, either divide the children into 4 groups (more supportive for shy children) or have 4 children demonstrate taking turns whilst playing on different instruments.

> Let's sit in four groups.
> One group is *sticks*, for running feet.
> One group is *sandblocks*, for running upstairs.
> One group is *bells*, for tapping on windows.
> One group is a *chime bar/cymbal/triangle" for a clock.
> You can only play your instrument when we sing about you.
> Let's practice running through the town.
> What about going upstairs and downstairs?
> Can we hear some tapping on windows and locks?
> And can we please hear 8 chimes of the clock?
> Let's get ready to play!

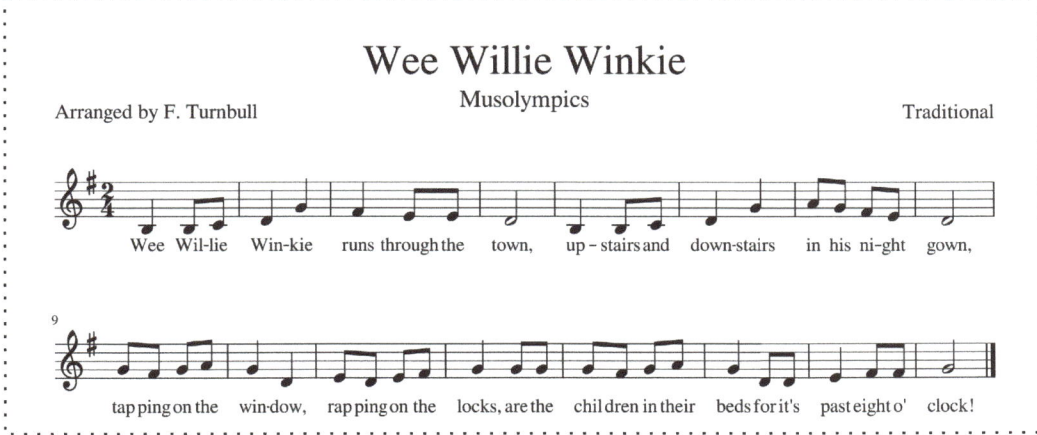

SPACE Statement

Social: Socially we stand and talk to friends in a circle, allowing us to interact with everyone equally - sitting in a circle does the same.

Physical: Modelling actions or tapping a beat enhances learning by using more senses.

Academic: Introducing new words develops vocabulary as well as other subjects like geography, history and science.

Creative: Exploring instruments and finding different ways to play them develops problem solving ideas.

Emotional: Singing together calms people by regulating the heartbeat.

Nursery Week 5&6

Here we come
Vocal Warm Up

What you will need:

Week 5:   Sticks

Week 6:   Parallel line dance

Focus: Turn-taking

This game in parallel lines develops turn-taking skills, following rules so that we all know when to sing and where to move.

Some running races are called relays.
You can only run once the other person has given you their baton or stick.
We're going to do a musical relay.
Let's stand up in two lines opposite each other.
First side 1 taps: tap, tap
Then side 2: tap, tap
Then side 1: tap, tap, tap, tap
Then side 2: tap, tap, tap, tap
Then we cross over - and swap sticks with someone.
Now we have a new side 1!
Let's play our game!

Here we come — Musolympics — Arranged by F. Turnbull — Traditional

Here we come! Where from? Bol-ton! What's your trade?
Cot-ton mills and le-mo-nade Give us some if you're not a-fraid!

SPACE Statement

Social: Socially we stand and talk to friends in a circle, allowing us to interact with everyone equally - sitting in a circle does the same.

Physical: Modelling actions or tapping a beat enhances learning by using more senses.

Academic: Introducing new words develops vocabulary as well as other subjects like geography, history and science.

Creative: Exploring instruments and finding different ways to play them develops problem solving ideas.

Emotional: Singing together calms people by regulating the heartbeat.

MUSICALITI NURSERY: RUN, HOP, SKIP

Nursery Week 5&6

Down came my friend

Movement

What you will need:

Week 5 and 6: None

Focus: Turn-taking and creative movement

This song develops performance and independence without the pressure, because it is a game! By standing in two rows and clapping, children learn to wait and watch, as the head couple walks down the centre. By walking down the centre, children have the opportunity to skip or dance as part of the game!

We're going to play another relay race game, but this time,
you can choose to dance or skip with your friend!
Let's stand in two lines opposite our friend, and clap:
clap, clap, clap, clap, clap, clap, clap, clap
This time when we clap, the friends at the end walk
in the middle to end of the lines, skipping or dancing.
Let's clap while they skip or dance:
clap, clap, clap, clap, clap, clap, clap, clap
They go to the end of the lines,
and now we have a new head couple to skip or dance!
Let's play our game!

SPACE Statement

Social: Socially we stand and talk to friends in a circle, allowing us to interact with everyone equally - sitting in a circle does the same.

Physical: Modelling actions or tapping a beat enhances learning by using more senses.

Academic: Introducing new words develops vocabulary as well as other subjects like geography, history and science.

Creative: Exploring instruments and finding different ways to play them develops problem solving ideas.

Emotional: Singing together calms people by regulating the heartbeat.

Nursery Week 5&6

Jolly Miller
Instrumental Play

What you will need:

Week 5: Multi-instruments

Week 6: Circle dance

Focus: Passing instruments after a phrase

In week 5, children play multi-instruments, practising playing and passing at the end of each line. In week 6, they could do the circle dance – on the last line, they choose a friend, hold their hands, and jump up and down!

We're going to play relay-racing with instruments this week!
After every music line, we pass to the left.
Let's practise: play, play, play, play, play, play, PASS.
Did you pass?
Let's try again: play, play, play, play, play, play, PASS.

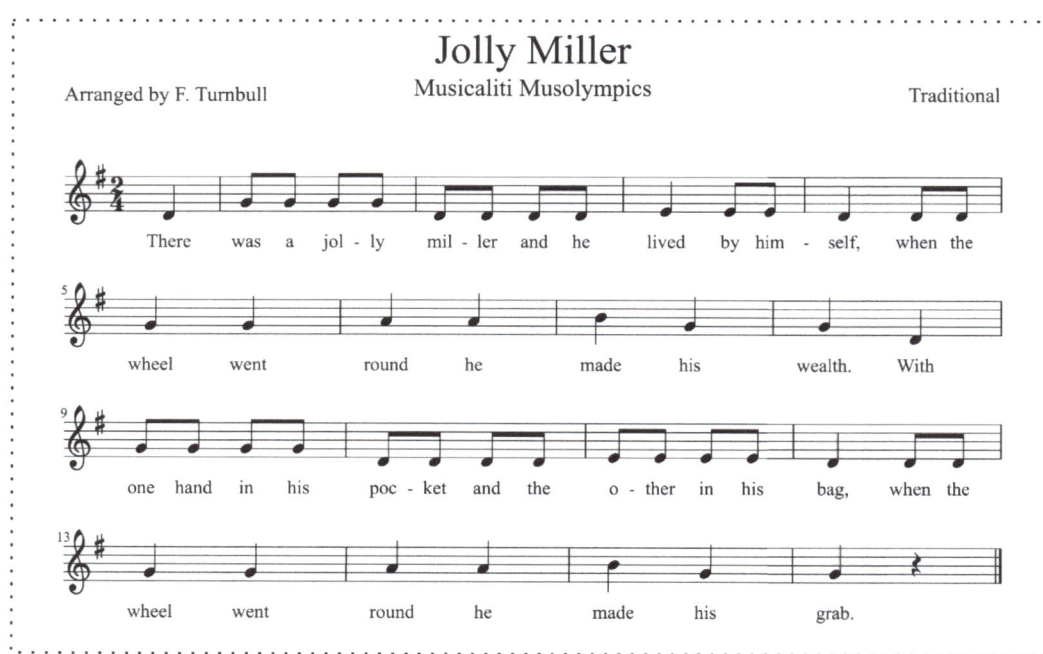

SPACE Statement

Social: Socially we stand and talk to friends in a circle, allowing us to interact with everyone equally – sitting in a circle does the same.

Physical: Modelling actions or tapping a beat enhances learning by using more senses.

Academic: Introducing new words develops vocabulary as well as other subjects like geography, history and science.

Creative: Exploring instruments and finding different ways to play them develops problem solving ideas.

Emotional: Singing together calms people by regulating the heartbeat.

MUSICALITI NURSERY: RUN, HOP, SKIP

Nursery Week 5 & 6

Athletics

Story/Investigation

What you will need:

Week 5 and 6:   Pictures and characters

* Reading each line slowly, encourage children to act out the story.

Are you ready to listen?
Each week learn about an olympic sport.
Have you been running?
Let's rub our ears and get them ready to listen.

Athletics was the first sport to be held at the Olympics.
Since 776BC, running has been a large part of European fairs.
Other examples of athletics can be found in the
Irish Tailteann and Scotlands' Highland Games.

Women were first included in the sport in 1928.
Now they compete in almost as many programmes as men.

Historically, American men have been the top champions,
challenged only by the USSR and East Germany.

Now many Caribbean countries are challenging them,
while Olympians from African states
dominate the distance events.

SPACE Statement

Social: Socially we stand and talk to friends in a circle, allowing us to interact with everyone equally - sitting in a circle does the same.

Physical: Modelling actions or tapping a beat enhances learning by using more senses.

Academic: Introducing new words develops vocabulary as well as other subjects like geography, history and science.

Creative: Exploring instruments and finding different ways to play them develops problem solving ideas.

Emotional: Singing together calms people by regulating the heartbeat.

Nursery Week 5&6

Athletics
Instrumental

What you will need:

Week 5: No equipment required
Track length: 0.31 (Ecossaise in E flat, K.MacCleod)

This time is for creative expression without talking. Demonstrate different ways to enjoy music without running or moving in a circle. Find different ways to express building up to the crescendo in the second part. Through free dance, we allow children to explore their own individual movement signature without imposing our own sense or style on them. Read about athletics for movement inspiration.

Listen for loud/quiet, high/low, fast/slow sounds and express them.

Week 6: No equipment required
Track length: 2.01 (Hustle, K. MacCleod)

This time is for creative expression without talking. Demonstrate responding to a change in key by starting with skipping, then clapping and knee-tapping when the music changes, then back to skipping. Look at pictures about running for movement inspiration.

Listen for pauses and clearly respond to them.

It's time to listen to music
and find a creative way to respond.
Be sure to listen to how the music sounds,
whether it is high or low, quick or slow,
and try to copy it.
Let's find lots of different ways
to respond to the music.

SPACE Statement

Social: Socially we stand and talk to friends in a circle, allowing us to interact with everyone equally - sitting in a circle does the same.

Physical: Modelling actions or tapping a beat enhances learning by using more senses.

Academic: Introducing new words develops vocabulary as well as other subjects like geography, history and science.

Creative: Exploring instruments and finding different ways to play them develops problem solving ideas.

Emotional: Singing together calms people by regulating the heartbeat.

MUSICALITI NURSERY: RUN, HOP, SKIP

Nursery Week 5 & 6

Goodbye

Goodbye Song

What you will need:

Week 1 and 2: Sit in circle to sing goodbye.

The recording can be used when singing to younger children who won't sing back yet. Stop after "but now it's time to say" so that you can sing to each child, and wait for them to sing back their response. This is a perfect opportunity to determine whether children are singing in tune on their own.

If stickers have been used as rewards for behaviour during the session, this is also the time to ensure that each child receives a sticker, showing each child that you value them equally.

What an exciting day we've had,
getting fit with athletics!
It's time to go, so let's get our
waving hands ready
as we get ready to sing goodbye.

SPACE Statement

Social: Socially we stand and talk to friends in a circle, allowing us to interact with everyone equally - sitting in a circle does the same.

Physical: Modelling actions or tapping a beat enhances learning by using more senses.

Academic: Introducing new words develops vocabulary as well as other subjects like geography, history and science.

Creative: Exploring instruments and finding different ways to play them develops problem solving ideas.

Emotional: Singing together calms people by regulating the heartbeat.

Goodbye my Friends
Arranged by F. Turnbull — Written by F. Turnbull

Good-bye my friends, good-bye, we've had a love-ly day, we love to sing and dance and play, but now it's time to say:
Good-bye (name) Good-bye (name) Good-bye (name) we've had a love-ly day.

4 Canoeing

Olympics

The Olympics are held every 4 years in different countries. This syllabus invites adults to look at the last Olympic results of their own country or countries represented by their children, and recognise the highest achieving individuals. Children may find the winners stories interesting, particularly finding out more about their childhood start in the sport, their family circumstances growing up, and outside jobs or interests.

Canoeing

Canoeing has been an Olympic sport since 1936. Canoes and kayaks were first used by South and North American Indians and Eskimos for transport, fishing and fighting. They moved through the water with a single bladed paddle made from wood.

In order to compete in flatwater events, the paddler must face forwards; the paddle must not be attached tot he boat; and it must be entirely powered with human energy.

Flatwater canoeing requires a calm water surface. Winners of this event usually come from Europe.

Rocking

Rocking is a time-honoured soothing technique, with success attributed to the gentle rocking originally experienced in the safety of the womb. There is a level of reassurance that appears to come from rocking at all ages, noticeable with those who struggle with balance, which may have something to do with the vestibular system based on the fluid in the inner ear. Creating opportunities to safely rock children can be tricky, and even the potential of rocking children in blankets can have varying levels of success, so it is best to be sensitive to each child's response.

F S TURNBULL

Whispering Voice
Hello Song

What you will need:

Masking tape music spots for sitting places.
Instruments and equipment out of reach.
Cover distractions with fabric.

Welcome children to Musicaliti!
Shall we practise our whispering voices:
(whisper) Do you have your whispering voice?
Let's practise our speaking voices:
(speak aloud) Do you have your speaking voice?
What about your singing voice:
(sing) Do you have your singing voice?
I think we're ready to begin!

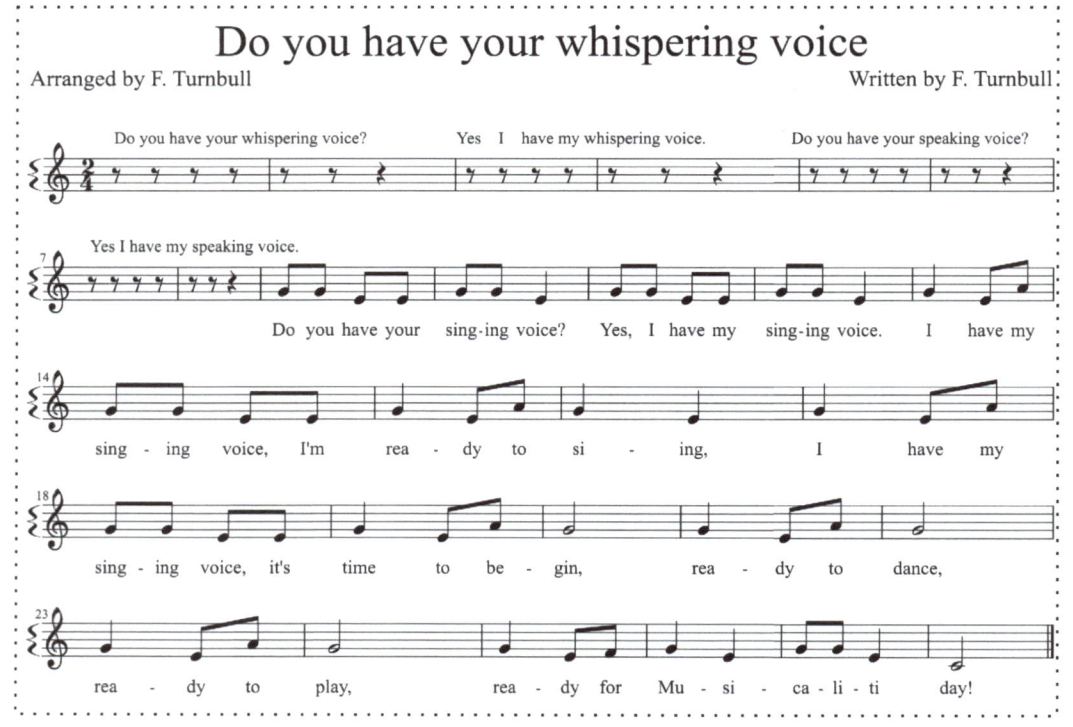

Nursery Week 7&8

SPACE Statement

Social: Socially we stand and talk to friends in a circle, allowing us to interact with everyone equally - sitting in a circle does the same.

Physical: Modelling actions or tapping a beat enhances learning by using more senses.

Academic: Introducing new words develops vocabulary as well as other subjects like geography, history and science.

Creative: Exploring instruments and finding different ways to play them develops problem solving ideas.

Emotional: Singing together calms people by regulating the heartbeat.

MUSICALITI NURSERY: RUN, HOP, SKIP

Nursery Week 7&8

Row your boat
Physical Warm Up

What you will need:

Week 7 and 8:   Triangles and "secret instruments"

Focus: Sound qualities of instruments

Recognising the different sounds that different instruments make is an introduction musically to timbre (instruments voices) as well as qualities or properties of materials (science). Have children take turns playing the triangle and then on or after the word dream, play a different instrument and have them guess what you played (tambourine, drum, maraca, guiro).

We're learning about canoeing, so we're going to sing
Row, Row, Row your Boat!
Today, we're going to take turns playing with a triangle.
Does it make a long or short sound?
That's right, it sounds long!
At the end of the song I am going to play a surprise
instrument behind my back.
Can you guess what this is?
Let's play!

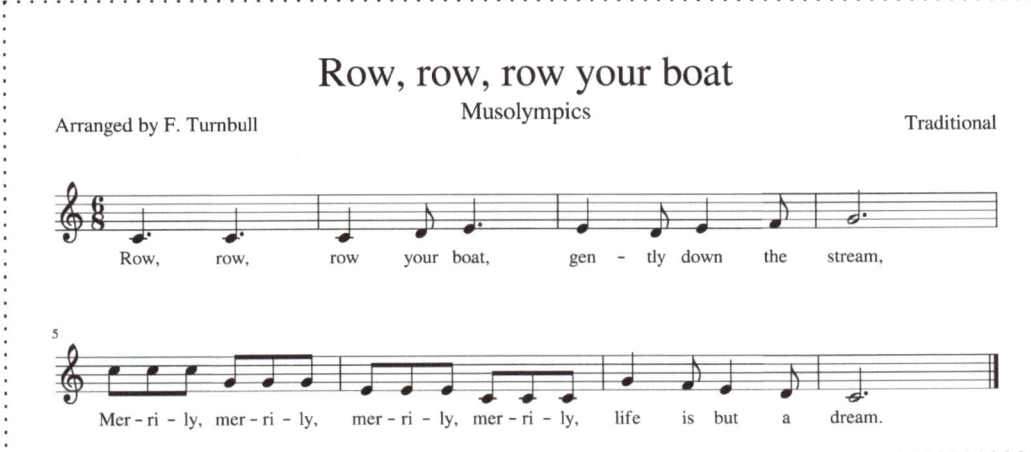

SPACE Statement

Social: Socially we stand and talk to friends in a circle, allowing us to interact with everyone equally - sitting in a circle does the same.

Physical: Modelling actions or tapping a beat enhances learning by using more senses.

Academic: Introducing new words develops vocabulary as well as other subjects like geography, history and science.

Creative: Exploring instruments and finding different ways to play them develops problem solving ideas.

Emotional: Singing together calms people by regulating the heartbeat.

F S TURNBULL

Rock a bye baby
Vocal Warm Up

What you will need:

Week 7: Parachute

Week 8: Strong blanket

Focus: Note duration, group co-operation.

This rocking lullaby gives children the opportunity to practise rocking a toy together in the parachute, and then the following week, having a turn themselves – 2 adults required to hold either end of blanket, and another to supervise the others!

Sometimes being on water can feel very relaxing,
like you're being rocked to sleep.
We're going to all hold onto a parachute and practise gently rocking our favourite toys on it.
Gently rock, gently rock, gently rock, gently rock.
Lovely.
Next week, you can have a turn in a strong blanket,
and we can gently rock, gently rock, gently rock, gently rock.
Let's play!

Nursery Week 7&8

SPACE Statement

Social: Socially we stand and talk to friends in a circle, allowing us to interact with everyone equally - sitting in a circle does the same.

Physical: Modelling actions or tapping a beat enhances learning by using more senses.

Academic: Introducing new words develops vocabulary as well as other subjects like geography, history and science.

Creative: Exploring instruments and finding different ways to play them develops problem solving ideas.

Emotional: Singing together calms people by regulating the heartbeat.

MUSICALITI NURSERY: RUN, HOP, SKIP

Nursery Week 7&8

See Saw, up and down

Pattern Dance

What you will need:

Week 7:   Sitting one behind another, like rowing a boat

Week 8:   Drum

Focus: Rhythm, sharing, synchronising

In the 7th week, we practise sitting like we're all in a long canoe, leaning forward and back, with the pulse of the song. In the 8th week, we tap the rhythm (beat of the words) with a drum, and take turns by passing it on.

When we sing Row, Row, Row Your Boat,
we usually sit opposite each other, don't we?
We pull our friend up, and they pull us up.
For See Saw, up and down, we're all going to sit
as if we're in a long, long canoe,
next to each other, with our legs apart,
facing the same way.
We all start by leaning forward as we sing, then lean back:
forward, back, forward, back, forward, back.
Next week, we'll use a drum
to tap the beat and pass it on,
but this week, let's all canoe, up and down!

SPACE Statement

Social: Socially we stand and talk to friends in a circle, allowing us to interact with everyone equally - sitting in a circle does the same.

Physical: Modelling actions or tapping a beat enhances learning by using more senses.

Academic: Introducing new words develops vocabulary as well as other subjects like geography, history and science.

Creative: Exploring instruments and finding different ways to play them develops problem solving ideas.

Emotional: Singing together calms people by regulating the heartbeat.

See Saw — Musolympics
Arranged by F. Turnbull — Traditional

See saw, up and down, in the sky and on the ground.

Nursery Week 7&8

This way Valerie
Instrumental Play

What you will need:

Week 7: Line dance

Week 8: Multi-instruments

Focus: Turn-taking

Standing in parallel lines, children take individual turns to dance down the centre, and the second child copies the first. In the 8th week, pass around instruments and all take turns playing each one by passing to the left at the end of each verse.

Let's stand in two lines, opposite our friend.
Decide who wants to be first, and who wants to go afterwards.
We'll start at one end, and the first person
rows their canoe down to the end of the line
while we sing "This way Valerie".
Then their friend copies them while we sing the next part.
Are you ready to play?
Next week, we'll take turns playing different instruments.

This Way Valerie — Musicaliti Musolympics
Arranged by F. Turnbull — Traditional

This way, Valerie, that way, Valerie, this way, Valerie, all day long.
Here come another one, just like the other one, here comes another one all day long.

SPACE Statement

Social: Socially we stand and talk to friends in a circle, allowing us to interact with everyone equally - sitting in a circle does the same.

Physical: Modelling actions or tapping a beat enhances learning by using more senses.

Academic: Introducing new words develops vocabulary as well as other subjects like geography, history and science.

Creative: Exploring instruments and finding different ways to play them develops problem solving ideas.

Emotional: Singing together calms people by regulating the heartbeat.

Nursery Week 7 & 8

Canoeing
Story/Investigation

What you will need:

Week 7 and 8:   Pictures and characters

* Reading each line slowly, encourage children to act out the story.

Are you ready to listen?
Each week learn about an olympic sport.
Have you been rowing?
Let's rub our ears and get them ready to listen.

Canoeing has been an Olympic sport since 1936.
Canoes and kayaks were first used by
South and North American Indians and Eskimos for
transport, fishing and fighting.
They moved through the water with a single bladed paddle
made from wood.

In order to compete in flatwater events,
the paddler must face forwards;
the paddle must not be attached tot he boat;
and it must be entirely powered with human energy.

Flatwater canoeing requires a calm water surface.
Winners of this event usually come from Europe.

SPACE Statement

Social: Socially we stand and talk to friends in a circle, allowing us to interact with everyone equally - sitting in a circle does the same.

Physical: Modelling actions or tapping a beat enhances learning by using more senses.

Academic: Introducing new words develops vocabulary as well as other subjects like geography, history and science.

Creative: Exploring instruments and finding different ways to play them develops problem solving ideas.

Emotional: Singing together calms people by regulating the heartbeat.

Nursery Week 7 & 8

Canoeing
Instrumental

What you will need:

Week 7: No equipment required
Track length: 2.00 (Dance of the sugar plum fairy, K.MacCleod)

This time is for creative expression without talking. Play the body using a variety of taps, claps, steps and stomps. The music is in 4/4 time so tap in time to the music and only change to tapping in a new position after a count of 4. Read about canoeing for movement inspiration.

Contrast loud/quiet, high/low, fast/slow sounds and express them.

Week 8: No equipment required
Track length: 2.47 (Digya, K. MacCleod)

This time is for creative expression without talking. Tap to the rhythm of the tune, or another simple rhythm, e.g. tap-tap-tap, tap-tap-tap. Look at pictures on canoeing for movement inspiration. The rhythm is the tune that the song follows (usually lyrics), and may be quicker or slower than the beat or pulse (constant beat).

It's time to listen to music
and find a creative way to respond.
Be sure to listen to how the music sounds,
whether it is high or low, quick or slow,
and try to copy it.
Let's find lots of different ways
to respond to the music.

SPACE Statement

Social: Socially we stand and talk to friends in a circle, allowing us to interact with everyone equally - sitting in a circle does the same.

Physical: Modelling actions or tapping a beat enhances learning by using more senses.

Academic: Introducing new words develops vocabulary as well as other subjects like geography, history and science.

Creative: Exploring instruments and finding different ways to play them develops problem solving ideas.

Emotional: Singing together calms people by regulating the heartbeat.

MUSICALITI NURSERY: RUN, HOP, SKIP

Nursery Week 7&8

Goodbye

Goodbye Song

What you will need:

Week 1 and 2:   Sit in circle to sing goodbye.

The recording can be used when singing to younger children who won't sing back yet. Stop after "but now it's time to say" so that you can sing to each child, and wait for them to sing back their response. This is a perfect opportunity to determine whether children are singing in tune on their own.

If stickers have been used as rewards for behaviour during the session, this is also the time to ensure that each child receives a sticker, showing each child that you value them equally.

What an exciting day we've had,
learning more about canoeing!
It's time to go, so let's get our
waving hands ready
as we get ready to sing goodbye.

SPACE Statement

Social: Socially we stand and talk to friends in a circle, allowing us to interact with everyone equally - sitting in a circle does the same.

Physical: Modelling actions or tapping a beat enhances learning by using more senses.

Academic: Introducing new words develops vocabulary as well as other subjects like geography, history and science.

Creative: Exploring instruments and finding different ways to play them develops problem solving ideas.

Emotional: Singing together calms people by regulating the heartbeat.

5 Gymnastics

Olympics

The Olympics are held every 4 years in different countries. This syllabus invites adults to look at the last Olympic results of their own country or countries represented by their children, and recognise the highest achieving individuals. Children may find the winners stories interesting, particularly finding out more about their childhood start in the sport, their family circumstances growing up, and outside jobs or interests.

Gymnastics

'Gymnos" is Greek for naked, as gymnasts used to wear no clothes when competing. Since then, the Federation Internationale de Gymnastique (FIG) was formed in 1881, and is recognised on 5 continents. It represents 3 areas of gymnastics:

- Artistic

- Rhythmic

- Trampoline

Artistic gymnastics is one of the best examples of an Olympic event performed on an apparatus, and only once ever has anyone achieved a perfect 10 seven times: 14-year-old Nadia Comeneci, from Romania, in 1976.

Weaving

Movement in this chapter is focussed on children standing in a circle, learning to physically weave. Choosing one child, have them work their way between children, in and out of the circle, until everyone finishes singing the song and they swap places with the child they are nearest. This is a fantastic gross motor experience of the later find motor co-ordination experience of sewing, which is why it is beneficial that children thread in and out between each child instead of running across the circle or only choosing to swap with their friends.

F S TURNBULL

Nursery Week 9 & 10

Whispering Voice

Hello Song

What you will need:

Masking tape music spots for sitting places.
Instruments and equipment out of reach.
Cover distractions with fabric.

Welcome children to Musicaliti!
Shall we practise our whispering voices:
(whisper) Do you have your whispering voice?
Let's practise our speaking voices:
(speak aloud) Do you have your speaking voice?
What about your singing voice:
(sing) Do you have your singing voice?
I think we're ready to begin!

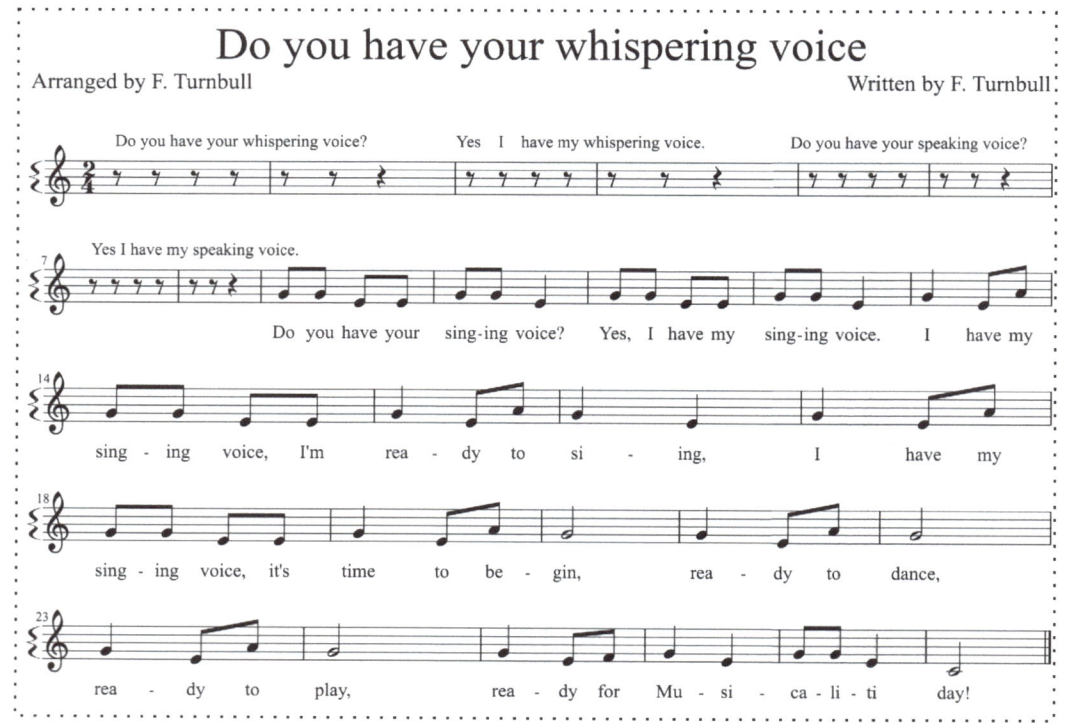

SPACE Statement

Social: Socially we stand and talk to friends in a circle, allowing us to interact with everyone equally - sitting in a circle does the same.

Physical: Modelling actions or tapping a beat enhances learning by using more senses.

Academic: Introducing new words develops vocabulary as well as other subjects like geography, history and science.

Creative: Exploring instruments and finding different ways to play them develops problem solving ideas.

Emotional: Singing together calms people by regulating the heartbeat.

MUSICALITI NURSERY: RUN, HOP, SKIP

Nursery Week 9&10

Ring a Rosies
Physical Warm Up

What you will need:

Week 9 and 10: Circle dance

Focus: Moving intentionally

Through the concept of gymnastics, we focus on intentional movement, deliberately "beautiful" movements while playing the familiar game, Ring a Rosies.

SPACE Statement

Social: Socially we stand and talk to friends in a circle, allowing us to interact with everyone equally - sitting in a circle does the same.

Physical: Modelling actions or tapping a beat enhances learning by using more senses.

Academic: Introducing new words develops vocabulary as well as other subjects like geography, history and science.

Creative: Exploring instruments and finding different ways to play them develops problem solving ideas.

Emotional: Singing together calms people by regulating the heartbeat.

Gymnastics is all about moving in beautiful ways.
Shall we stand up and make a circle?
Holding hands, let's walk around.
I'm sure you'll know this song as soon as it starts,
"Ring a Ring a Rosies"!
This time as we sing it, let's pretend that we are
famous gymnasts, and we always move beautifully.
When we walk around the circle, let's walk beautifully.
When we fall down, let's fall down beautifully.
And when we stand up, let's stand up …
beautifully!

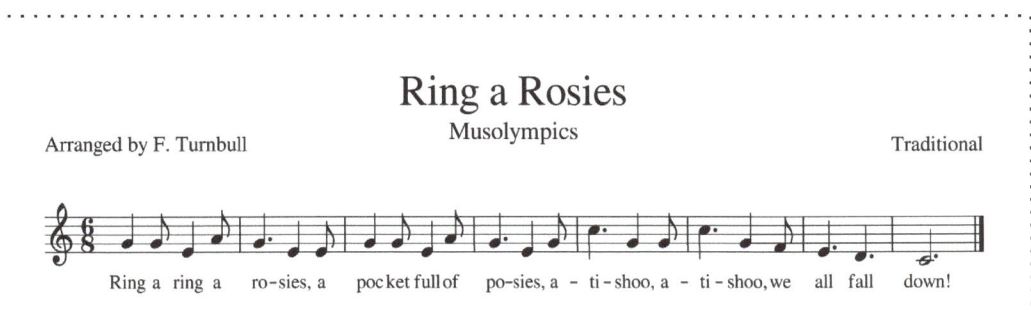

Ring a Rosies
Musolympics
Arranged by F. Turnbull   Traditional

Ring a ring a ro-sies, a pocket full of po-sies, a-ti-shoo, a-ti-shoo, we all fall down!

F S TURNBULL

What shall we do?
Vocal Warm Up

What you will need:

Week 9 and 10:   Hoops/boxes/plastic pipes etc.

Focus: Exploratory play

Using everyday materials, get the children to create a pretend playground with things like swings, see-saws, climbing frames etc. Deliberately using non-descript items like boxes helps children to build their imaginative skills and confidence.

Look at all of these different things here.
Could we pretend to make a playground from them?
What could we use as a swing? A slide? A seesaw?
What great ideas!
Let's have a walk around everything as we sing our song,
and then we'll choose something to be a see saw,
and a climbing frame!
Who knows what else we may find!

**Nursery
Week 9&10**

SPACE Statement

Social:
Socially we stand and talk to friends in a circle, allowing us to interact with everyone equally - sitting in a circle does the same.

Physical:
Modelling actions or tapping a beat enhances learning by using more senses.

Academic:
Introducing new words develops vocabulary as well as other subjects like geography, history and science.

Creative:
Exploring instruments and finding different ways to play them develops problem solving ideas.

Emotional:
Singing together calms people by regulating the heartbeat.

MUSICALITI NURSERY: RUN, HOP, SKIP

Around the buttercup
Movement

What you will need:

Week 9 & 10: Scarf/ribbon

Focus: Weaving, gross motor co-ordination

Standing in a circle, children take turns weaving in and out in between each child. This is a great pre-curser to the fine co-ordination skill of sewing.

Nursery Week 9 & 10

SPACE Statement

Social: Socially we stand and talk to friends in a circle, allowing us to interact with everyone equally - sitting in a circle does the same.

Physical: Modelling actions or tapping a beat enhances learning by using more senses.

Academic: Introducing new words develops vocabulary as well as other subjects like geography, history and science.

Creative: Exploring instruments and finding different ways to play them develops problem solving ideas.

Emotional: Singing together calms people by regulating the heartbeat.

Gymnasts use different things when they move,
sometimes balls, scarves or ribbons.
We're going to move like gymnasts with ribbons
by pretending to sew.
Do you know how to sew?
That's right, the needle goes into the material
and then out again, leaving a thread
that makes a pattern and holds the material together.
We're going to use a long scarf or ribbon
to walk in between our friends as we sing our song.
On the last line, we swap with the last person
nearest the ribbon, and give them a turn to "sew"!

All around the buttercup
Musolympics
Arranged by F. Turnbull
Traditional

All a-round the but-ter cup, one, two three, if you want an awe-some friend, just choose me.

Nursery Week 9 & 10

Skip to my Lou

Instrumental Play

What you will need:

Week 9: Skipping

Week 10: Bells

Focus: Skipping, jingling to the beat

This is a great song to teach the foundations of skipping easily to all.

Gymnasts do a lot of complicated movements but one that we can easily copy is skipping.
Hop on one foot: hop, hop, hop, hop.
Now hop on the other: hop, hop, hop, hop.
Let's do two hops now: hop, hop.
Swap feet, and hop twice: hop, hop.
Let's keep hopping twice and swapping as we move around the room. Next week, we'll jingle!

SPACE Statement

Social: Socially we stand and talk to friends in a circle, allowing us to interact with everyone equally – sitting in a circle does the same.

Physical: Modelling actions or tapping a beat enhances learning by using more senses.

Academic: Introducing new words develops vocabulary as well as other subjects like geography, history and science.

Creative: Exploring instruments and finding different ways to play them develops problem solving ideas.

Emotional: Singing together calms people by regulating the heartbeat.

MUSICALITI NURSERY: RUN, HOP, SKIP

Nursery Week 9&10

Gymnastics
Story/Investigation

What you will need:

Week 9 and 10:   Pictures and characters

* Reading each line slowly, encourage children to act out the story.

Are you ready to listen?
Each week learn about an olympic sport.
Have you done gymnastics?
Let's rub our ears and get them ready to listen.

'Gymnos" is Greek for naked,
as gymnasts used to wear no clothes when competing.
Since then,
the Federation Internationale de Gymnastique (FIG)
was formed in 1881,
and is recognised on 5 continents.

It represents 3 areas of gymnastics:
- Artistic
- Rhythmic
- Trampoline

Artistic gymnastics is one of the best examples of an
Olympic event performed on an apparatus,
and only once ever has anyone achieved a perfect 10 seven times:
14-year-old Nadia Comeneci, from Romania, in 1976.

SPACE Statement

Social: Socially we stand and talk to friends in a circle, allowing us to interact with everyone equally - sitting in a circle does the same.

Physical: Modelling actions or tapping a beat enhances learning by using more senses.

Academic: Introducing new words develops vocabulary as well as other subjects like geography, history and science.

Creative: Exploring instruments and finding different ways to play them develops problem solving ideas.

Emotional: Singing together calms people by regulating the heartbeat.

Nursery Week 9 & 10

Gymnastics
Instrumental

What you will need:

Week 9: Scarves
Track length: 1.44 (Egmont Oversture Finale, K. McCleod)

This time is for creative expression without talking. Begin by clapping along with the main music line in this song. Use this song and choose which instrument line you wish to follow, violins or bass, as these are at different tempi (one is slower than the other). Read more about gymnastics for movement inspiration.

Week 10: Scarves
Track length: 2.33 (Thaxted, K. MacCleod)

This time is for creative expression without talking. This blues-style music has a strong beat with creative improvisation throughout. Choose which level you want to work with the group, keeping the regular beat (e.g. by walking or stamping), and making up your own movements towards improvising (e.g. with scarves or arms). Look at pictures of gymnastics for movement inspiration.

It's time to listen to music
and find a creative way to respond.
Be sure to listen to how the music sounds,
whether it is high or low, quick or slow,
and try to copy it.
Let's find lots of different ways
to respond to the music.

SPACE Statement

Social: Socially we stand and talk to friends in a circle, allowing us to interact with everyone equally - sitting in a circle does the same.

Physical: Modelling actions or tapping a beat enhances learning by using more senses.

Academic: Introducing new words develops vocabulary as well as other subjects like geography, history and science.

Creative: Exploring instruments and finding different ways to play them develops problem solving ideas.

Emotional: Singing together calms people by regulating the heartbeat.

MUSICALITI NURSERY: RUN, HOP, SKIP

Nursery Week 9&10

Goodbye

Goodbye Song

What you will need:

Week 1 and 2:   Sit in circle to sing goodbye.

The recording can be used when singing to younger children who won't sing back yet. Stop after "but now it's time to say" so that you can sing to each child, and wait for them to sing back their response. This is a perfect opportunity to determine whether children are singing in tune on their own.

If stickers have been used as rewards for behaviour during the session, this is also the time to ensure that each child receives a sticker, showing each child that you value them equally.

What an exciting day we've had,
doing gymnastics!
It's time to go, so let's get our
waving hands ready
as we get ready to sing goodbye.

SPACE Statement

Social: Socially we stand and talk to friends in a circle, allowing us to interact with everyone equally - sitting in a circle does the same.

Physical: Modelling actions or tapping a beat enhances learning by using more senses.

Academic: Introducing new words develops vocabulary as well as other subjects like geography, history and science.

Creative: Exploring instruments and finding different ways to play them develops problem solving ideas.

Emotional: Singing together calms people by regulating the heartbeat.

6 Tennis

Olympics

The Olympics are held every 4 years in different countries. This syllabus invites adults to look at the last Olympic results of their own country or countries represented by their children, and recognise the highest achieving individuals. Children may find the winners stories interesting, particularly finding out more about their childhood start in the sport, their family circumstances growing up, and outside jobs or interests.

Tennis

Tennis has been part of the Olympics since 1896. At the first event, only men's singles and men's doubles were played, but since 1900, women have been allowed to play. It was stopped in 1924 because of a dispute with the International Lawn Tennis Federation, but returned again in 1988.

The playing surface can either be hard court, clay court or grass court. Players can enter men's singles or doubles, women's singles or doubles or mixed doubles.

Tennis is thought to have started as far back as the 11th century, becoming popular in England in the late 19th century. Historically, players from England and America have won this event.

Instrument Passing

Introducing instrument passing is useful, not only to help children experience patience, but also to develop their sense of timing and co-operation. By waiting for each person to have their turn, they find a way to constructively pass the time (singing and tapping), as well as watching through the example of the child playing the instrument to be passed. Patience, co-operation, and timing are all essential in life, from orchestras to business deals, and this is an enjoyable, fun way for children to all be involved.

F S TURNBULL

Nursery Week 11 & 12

Whispering Voice

Hello Song

What you will need:

Masking tape music spots for sitting places.
Instruments and equipment out of reach.
Cover distractions with fabric.

Welcome children to Musicaliti!
Shall we practise our whispering voices:
(whisper) Do you have your whispering voice?
Let's practise our speaking voices:
(speak aloud) Do you have your speaking voice?
What about your singing voice:
(sing) Do you have your singing voice?
I think we're ready to begin!

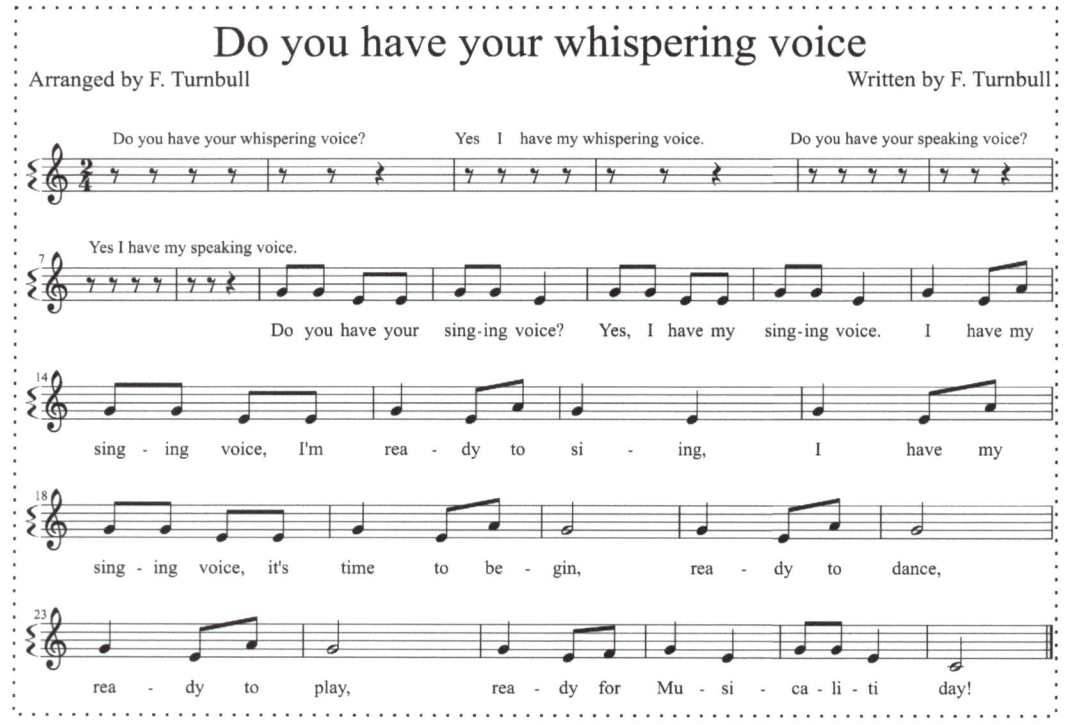

SPACE Statement

Social:
Socially we stand and talk to friends in a circle, allowing us to interact with everyone equally - sitting in a circle does the same.

Physical:
Modelling actions or tapping a beat enhances learning by using more senses.

Academic:
Introducing new words develops vocabulary as well as other subjects like geography, history and science.

Creative:
Exploring instruments and finding different ways to play them develops problem solving ideas.

Emotional:
Singing together calms people by regulating the heartbeat.

MUSICALITI NURSERY: RUN, HOP, SKIP

Nursery Week 11 & 12

Old brass wagon

Physical Warm Up

What you will need:

Week 11 & 12:   Circle dance

Focus: Listening and co-ordination

Children develop listening skills as they must move in response to the words they hear, while still being aware of keeping the space of the circle.

Tennis is great game that people play often in the summer,
and we play it with a tennis racquet and a … ball, that's right!
I love that balls can be so bouncy,
because they are round!
Let's sing a song about going around, like a ball.
Can you walk to the left? Walk, walk, walk, walk!
Can you walk to the right? Walk, walk, walk, walk!
Can you crouch low and then stand tall?
Crouch, stand, crouch, stand!
Can you walk to the middle of the circle, and then back out?
Let's play Old Brass Wagon!

SPACE Statement

Social: Socially we stand and talk to friends in a circle, allowing us to interact with everyone equally - sitting in a circle does the same.

Physical: Modelling actions or tapping a beat enhances learning by using more senses.

Academic: Introducing new words develops vocabulary as well as other subjects like geography, history and science.

Creative: Exploring instruments and finding different ways to play them develops problem solving ideas.

Emotional: Singing together calms people by regulating the heartbeat.

Bounce high

Vocal Warm Up

What you will need:

Week 11 & 12:   Balls

Focus: Turn-taking, responding to the first beat

By taking turns rolling the ball to each other, children learn to share, and trust. By getting children to only roll when they sing the word roll, children develop hearing and concentration skills to find the first beat (at the start of each line): "Roll .... Roll ... Roll ... Leicester ..."

What a lovely circle we're sitting in!
In tennis, one person hits the ball to the other,
and the other has to hit it back.
Let's pretend we're playing tennis!
Can you roll this ball back to me if I roll it to you? Lovely!
Now can you bounce it back to me? Great!
Sitting opposite our friend, we're all going to have a ball
to roll to each other, and then bounce to each other.
We can only "roll" or "bounce" when we hear that word,
so can we have a go?
Remember, we have to wait until we hear the word, "Roll".

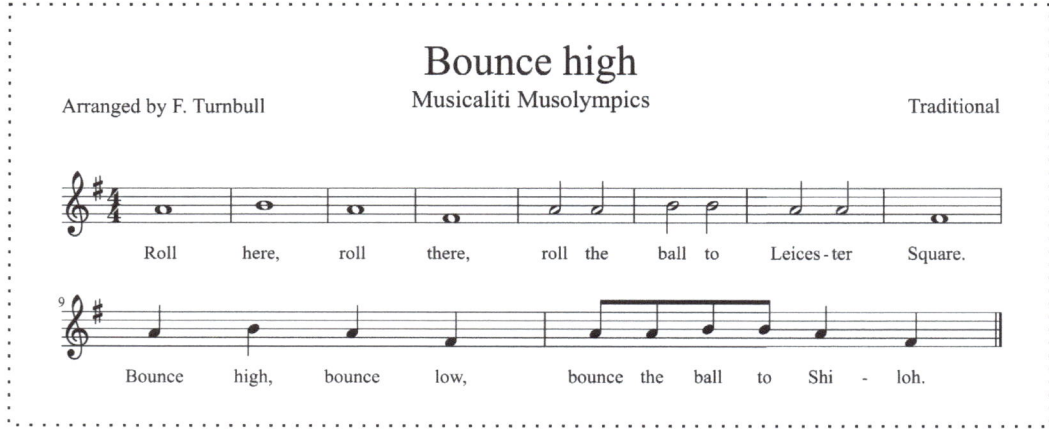

Bounce high
Musicaliti Musolympics
Arranged by F. Turnbull   Traditional

Roll here, roll there, roll the ball to Leices-ter Square.

Bounce high, bounce low, bounce the ball to Shi - loh.

SPACE Statement

Social: Socially we stand and talk to friends in a circle, allowing us to interact with everyone equally - sitting in a circle does the same.

Physical: Modelling actions or tapping a beat enhances learning by using more senses.

Academic: Introducing new words develops vocabulary as well as other subjects like geography, history and science.

Creative: Exploring instruments and finding different ways to play them develops problem solving ideas.

Emotional: Singing together calms people by regulating the heartbeat.

MUSICALITI NURSERY: RUN, HOP, SKIP

Nursery Week 11 & 12

Riding in a buggy

Pattern Dance

What you will need:

Week 11:   Ukulele

Week 12:   Flattened boxes

Focus: Turn-taking

In the 11th week, we take turns with the ukulele, passing and playing while we learn the song. In the 12th week, we use flattened cardboard boxes to pull friends around, pretending they are in prams, then swapping so we all have a turn.

> Tennis is all about taking turns to play.
> We're going to take turns to play this ukulele!
> Can you hear how long the sound lasts?
> Let's each have a turn while we sing our buggy song.
> Sometimes a baby pram can be called a baby buggy,
> which is the old word that we use in this song.
> As we sing, let's pass the ukulele to the next person,
> so that everyone can have a go.
> If it's not your turn, you can pat your knees.
> Next week, we will pull our friends around
> in pretend buggies!

SPACE Statement

Social: Socially we stand and talk to friends in a circle, allowing us to interact with everyone equally - sitting in a circle does the same.

Physical: Modelling actions or tapping a beat enhances learning by using more senses.

Academic: Introducing new words develops vocabulary as well as other subjects like geography, history and science.

Creative: Exploring instruments and finding different ways to play them develops problem solving ideas.

Emotional: Singing together calms people by regulating the heartbeat.

Riding in a buggy — Musicaliti Musolympics
Arranged by F. Turnbull — Traditional

Ri-ding in a bug-gy Miss Ma-ry Jane, Miss Ma-ry Jane, Miss Ma-ry Jane,
Ri-ding in a bug-gy Miss Ma-ry Jane, I'm a long way from home.

Rover red Rover

Instrument Play

What you will need:

Week 11 & 12: Xylophone (wood)/Glockenspiel (metal)

Focus: Instrument pass-around

This week we focus on taking turns as children explore the xylophone/glockenspiel. This is a fun instrument but it is helpful to learn to hold the beaters properly. Practically, this means holding the beaters like a spoon, to get the right sound (not like a fork). Lightly tap the bars to get a clear sound, ideally holding a beater in each hand.

> Let's take turns again with a new instrument.
> Look as this xylophone/glockenspiel.
> Does it make a long sound or a short sound?
> Let's each have a turn while we sing our Rover song.
> Children used to play this game by holding hands in a long line and calling someone over to try to break through someone's hands.
> Instead of breaking through hands, we're going to sing the name of the next person to play the xylophone/glockenspiel.

Nursery Week 11 & 12

SPACE Statement

Social: Socially we stand and talk to friends in a circle, allowing us to interact with everyone equally - sitting in a circle does the same.

Physical: Modelling actions or tapping a beat enhances learning by using more senses.

Academic: Introducing new words develops vocabulary as well as other subjects like geography, history and science.

Creative: Exploring instruments and finding different ways to play them develops problem solving ideas.

Emotional: Singing together calms people by regulating the heartbeat.

Rover Red Rover — Musicaliti Musolympics
Arranged by F. Turnbull — Traditional
Ro-ver, red Ro-ver, We call An-dy o-ver.

MUSICALITI NURSERY: RUN, HOP, SKIP

Nursery Week 11 & 12

Tennis

Story/Investigation

What you will need:

Week 11 and 12:   Pictures and characters

* Reading each line slowly, encourage children to act out the story.

Are you ready to listen?
Each week we learn about an olympic sport.
Have you played tennis?
Let's rub our ears and get them ready to listen.

> Tennis has been part of the Olympics since 1896.
> At the first event, only men's singles and men's doubles were played,
> but since 1900, women have been allowed to play.
> It was stopped in 1924 because of a dispute with the
> International Lawn Tennis Federation,
> but returned again in 1988.
>
> The playing surface can either be hard court,
> clay court or grass court.
>
> Players can enter men's singles or doubles,
> women's singles or doubles or mixed doubles.
> Tennis is thought to have started as far back as the 11th century,
> becoming popular in England in the late 19th century.
> Historically, players from England and America
> have won this event.

SPACE Statement

Social: Socially we stand and talk to friends in a circle, allowing us to interact with everyone equally - sitting in a circle does the same.

Physical: Modelling actions or tapping a beat enhances learning by using more senses.

Academic: Introducing new words develops vocabulary as well as other subjects like geography, history and science.

Creative: Exploring instruments and finding different ways to play them develops problem solving ideas.

Emotional: Singing together calms people by regulating the heartbeat.

Nursery Week 11 & 12

Tennis
Instrumental

What you will need:

Week 11: No equipment required
Track length: *choose an old/ new instrumental song*

This time is for creative expression without talking. Begin by clapping along with the main music line in this song.

Use this song and choose which type of instrument you wish to follow, violins or bass, as these are at different tempi (one beat is slower than the other). Read the more about tennis for movement inspiration.

Week 12: No equipment required
Track length: *choose and old/new instrumental song*

This time is for creative expression without talking. This blues-style music has a strong beat with creative improvisation throughout. Choose which level you want to work with the group, keeping the regular beat (e.g. by walking or stamping), and making up your own movements towards improvising (e.g. with scarves or arms). Look at pictures about tennis for movement inspiration.

It's time to listen to music
and find a creative way to respond.
Be sure to listen to how the music sounds,
whether it is high or low, quick or slow,
and try to copy it.
Let's find lots of different ways
to respond to the music.

SPACE Statement

Social: Socially we stand and talk to friends in a circle, allowing us to interact with everyone equally - sitting in a circle does the same.

Physical: Modelling actions or tapping a beat enhances learning by using more senses.

Academic: Introducing new words develops vocabulary as well as other subjects like geography, history and science.

Creative: Exploring instruments and finding different ways to play them develops problem solving ideas.

Emotional: Singing together calms people by regulating the heartbeat.

Goodbye

Goodbye Song

What you will need:

Week 11 and 12:   Sit in circle to sing goodbye.

The recording can be used when singing to younger children who won't sing back yet. Stop after "but now it's time to say" so that you can sing to each child, and wait for them to sing back their response. This is a perfect opportunity to determine whether children are singing in tune on their own.

If stickers have been used as rewards for behaviour during the session, this is also the time to ensure that each child receives a sticker, showing each child that you value them equally.

> What an exciting day we've had,
> finding out about and playing tennis!
> It's time to go, so let's get our
> waving hands ready
> as we get ready to sing goodbye.

SPACE Statement

Social: Socially we stand and talk to friends in a circle, allowing us to interact with everyone equally - sitting in a circle does the same.

Physical: Modelling actions or tapping a beat enhances learning by using more senses.

Academic: Introducing new words develops vocabulary as well as other subjects like geography, history and science.

Creative: Exploring instruments and finding different ways to play them develops problem solving ideas.

Emotional: Singing together calms people by regulating the heartbeat.

7 HANDOUTS

Why Handouts?

This series includes handouts sheets for each of the characters as a reminder of the music series this term. Pictures of the characters are included on the handouts next to the title, and the notes represented are also included so that children become familiar and more comfortable with music notation.

Handouts act as useful reminders for children and conversation points for parents of children who may be less vocal than others. Musically-trained parents may be able to pick out the tune, while non-musical parents will be able to read the words, potentially reminding their child of the tune. Children will certainly be reminded by the exciting story included with each handout. With most songs written in the anhemitonic pentatonic scale, songs extend only five notes (excluding notes with semi tones), making it easier for children to learn and sing successfully.

In addition to the handouts, a colour page of characters has been included and may be reproduced for storytelling, as well as an A4 colour picture, showing the sequence of the sports, as a background for the characters.

Notation practice

Musical knowledge may also be consolidated using the hand out sheets which may be photocopied. The 'Make your own rhythm' pages can be copied, cut and laminated so that children can create rhythms of songs they already sing, or to create new rhythms to clap or tap. The rhythm lines are in 4/4 time so that each line can have four counts (gaps are rests). The notation used on the lines may be musical or insect depending on the children.

A quick reminder of the notation values:

Semibreve/whole note	Swimming	4 counts	(1 on a line)
Minim/half note	Cycling	2 counts	(2 on a line)
Crotchet/quarter note	Canoeing	1 count	(4 on a line)
Quaver/eighth note	Athletics	1/2 count	(8 on a line)
Semiquaver/sixteenth note	Tennis	1/4 count	(16 on a line)
Dotted quaver semiquaver Dotted eighth note sixteenth note	Gymnastics	1 count	(4 on a line)

  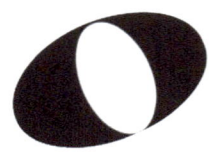

Swimming

Old Brass Wagon
Musicaliti Musolympics

Arranged by F. Turnbull · Traditional

Cir-cle to the left, old brass wa-gon, cir-cle to the left, old brass wa-gon,

cir-cle to the left, old brass wa-gon, you're the one, my dar-ling.

Bounce high
Musicaliti Musolympics

Arranged by F. Turnbull · Traditional

Roll here, roll there, roll the ball to Leices-ter Square.

Bounce high, bounce low, bounce the ball to Shi-loh.

MAY BE REPRODUCED FOR EDUCATIONAL PURPOSES ONLY

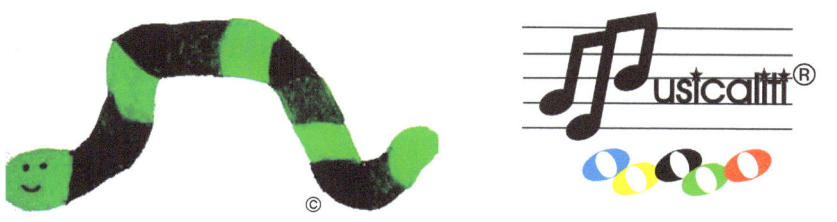
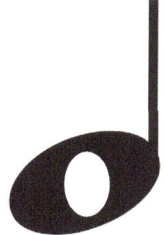

Cycling

Snail, snail
Musicaliti Musolympics

Arranged by F. Turnbull

Traditional

Snail, snail, snail, snail, creep a-round and round and round.

Babylon
Musicaliti Musolympics

Arranged by F. Turnbull

Traditional

A: How many miles to Ba-by-lon?   B: Three score and ten.

A: Will I get there be-fore you do?   B: Yes, and back a-gain!

A: O-pen the gates and let us through!   B: Not with-out a beck and bow!

A: Here's the beck!   B: Here's the bow!   A: O-pen the gates and let us through!

MAY BE REPRODUCED FOR EDUCATIONAL PURPOSES ONLY

Canoeing

See Saw
Musicaliti Musolympics

Arranged by F. Turnbull
Traditional

See - saw, up and down, in the sky and on the ground.

This Way Valerie
Musicaliti Musolympics

Arranged by F. Turnbull
Traditional

This way, Va-le-rie, that way, Va-le-rie, this way, Va-le-rie, all day long.

Here come a-no-ther one, just like the o-ther one, here comes a-no-ther one all day long.

MAY BE REPRODUCED FOR EDUCATIONAL PURPOSES ONLY

Athletics

Down came my friend
Musicaliti Musolympics

Arranged by F. Turnbull　　　　　　　　　　　　　　　　　　　　　　　Traditional

Down came my friend and down came two,
down came George's friend and he was dressed in blue.

Jolly Miller
Musicaliti Musolympics

Arranged by F. Turnbull　　　　　　　　　　　　　　　　　　　　　　　Traditional

There was a jol-ly mil-ler and he lived by him-self, when the wheel went round he made his wealth. With one hand in his poc-ket and the o-ther in his bag, when the wheel went round he made his grab.

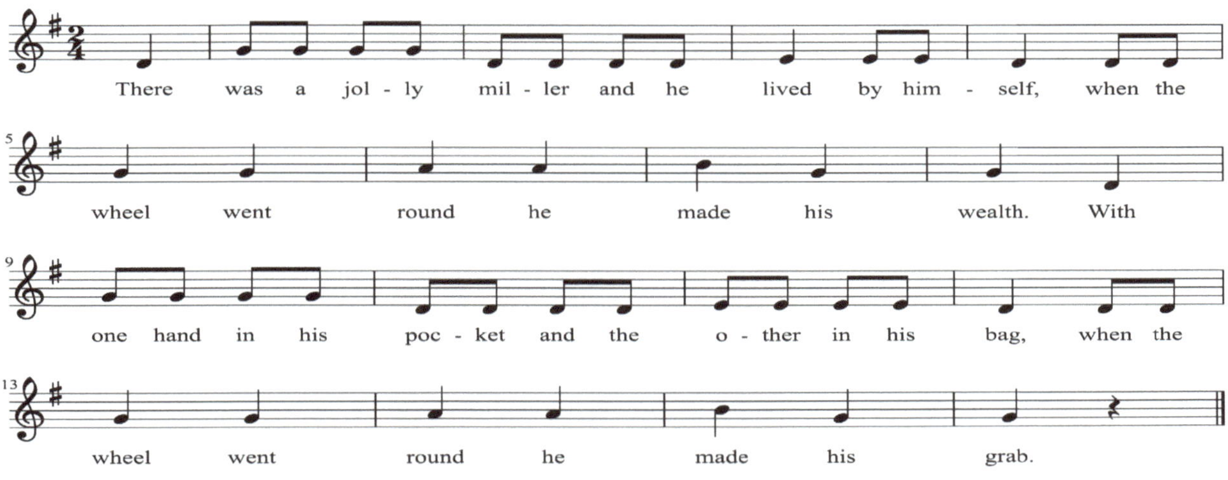

MAY BE REPRODUCED FOR EDUCATIONAL PURPOSES ONLY

Gymnastics

All around the buttercup

Arranged by F. Turnbull Musicaliti Musolympics Traditional

All a-round the but-ter-cup, one, two, three,

if you want a pret-ty friend, just choose me.

Skip to my Lou

Arranged by F. Turnbull Musicaliti Musolympics Traditional

Fly in the but-ter milk, shoo fly, shoo! Fly in the but-ter milk, shoo fly shoo!

Fly in the but-ter milk, shoo fly, shoo! Skip to my Lou, my dar-ling!

Skip, skip, skip to my Lou, skip, skip, skip to my Lou,

skip, skip, skip to my Lou, skip to my Lou, my dar-ling!

MAY BE REPRODUCED FOR EDUCATIONAL PURPOSES ONLY

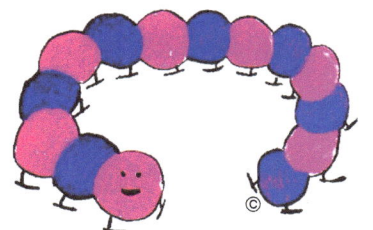 

Tennis

Riding in a buggy
Musicaliti Musolympics

Arranged by F. Turnbull
Traditional

Ri-ding in a bug-gy Miss Ma-ry jane, Miss Ma-ry Jane, Miss Ma-ry Jane,

Ri-ding in a bug-gy Miss Ma-ry Jane, I'm a long way from home.

Rover Red Rover
Musicaliti Musolympics

Arranged by F. Turnbull
Traditional

Ro - ver, red Ro - ver, We call An-dy o - ver.

MAY BE REPRODUCED FOR EDUCATIONAL PURPOSES ONLY

MUSICALITI NURSERY: RUN, HOP, SKIP

MAY BE REPRODUCED FOR EDUCATIONAL PURPOSES ONLY

Make your own Rhythms:

Cut out notes and insects and place them on the rhythm line.

MAY BE REPRODUCED FOR EDUCATIONAL PURPOSES ONLY

MUSICALITI NURSERY: RUN, HOP, SKIP

Make your own Rhythms:

Cut out notes and insects and place them on the rhythm line.

MAY BE REPRODUCED FOR EDUCATIONAL PURPOSES ONLY

Make your own Rhythms:

4
4

4
4

4
4

4
4

Cut out notes and insects and place them on the rhythm line.

MAY BE REPRODUCED FOR EDUCATIONAL PURPOSES ONLY

MUSICALITI NURSERY: RUN, HOP, SKIP

Make your own Rhythms:

4
4

4
4

4
4

4
4

Cut out notes and insects and place them on the rhythm line.

MAY BE REPRODUCED FOR EDUCATIONAL PURPOSES ONLY

Make your own Rhythms:

| 4 |
|4

|4
|4

|4
|4

|4
|4

Cut out notes and insects and place them on the rhythm line.

MAY BE REPRODUCED FOR EDUCATIONAL PURPOSES ONLY

F S TURNBULL

AVAILABLE TITLES:

Musicaliti Nursery: Round and Round is a full-colour, illustrated book of well known children's songs for children. Each song includes music rhythms to which children can clap, tap, walk and sing.

ISBN: 978-1-907-935-008

Musicaliti Nursery Series: Magical Musical Kingdom is a full-colour, teaching series of well known and original children's songs with a royal element. Sessions include suggested instruments and activities, with an optional CD of music to purchase or download.

ISBN: 978-1-907-935-152

Musicaliti Nursery Series: Yum, Yum, Yum! is a full-colour, teaching series of well known and original children's songs with a yummy food element. Sessions include suggested instruments and activities, with an optional CD of music to purchase or download.

ISBN: 978-1-907-935-206

FORTHCOMING TITLES:

Musicaliti Nursery Series: Car, bike, plane is a full-colour, teaching series of well known and original children's songs with a transport element. Sessions include suggested instruments and activities, with an optional CD of music to purchase or download.

ISBN: 978-1-907-935-213

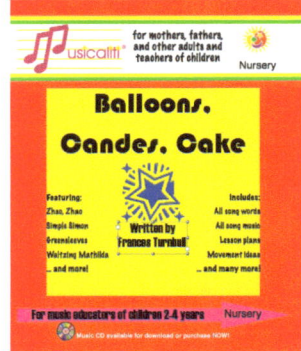

Musicaliti Nursery Series: Balloons, Candles, Cake is a full-colour, teaching series of well known and original children's songs with a party element. Sessions include suggested instruments and activities, with an optional CD of music to purchase or download.

ISBN: 978-1-907-935-190

Follow Musicaliti on Blogger, FaceBook, LinkedIn, Pintrest, ReverbNation, SoundCloud, Twitter, Wordpress & YouTube!

ABOUT THE AUTHOR

Frances has presented early years music sessions in a variety of settings since 2006, after training as a secondary mathematics and science teacher. She is fascinated by research into the health, educational and developmental benefits of music. Not content with being involved with children's music alone, she has a bachelor's degree in Psychology, master's degree in Education, teaches private primary guitar, and directs a local community choir, the Warblers.